# THE
# WEDDING
# PLANNER

FAMILY MATTERS

✓

# THE WEDDING PLANNER

**ANGELA LANSBURY**

WARD LOCK

First published 1990 by Ward Lock
Artillery House, Artillery Row, London SW1P 1RT, England

A Cassell imprint

© Text Ward Lock Limited 1990

© Illustrations Ward Lock Limited 1990

Text set by Columns of Reading
Illustrations by Michael Shoebridge
Printed and bound in Great Britain by
William Collins Sons & Co. Ltd., Glasgow

**British Library Cataloguing in Publication Data**
Lansbury, Angela
  The Wedding planner. – (Family matters)
  1. Wedding. Planning
  I. Title II. Series
  395'.22

ISBN 0–7063–6867–3

# CONTENTS

| INTRODUCTION | 8 |
| Being Well Organized | 8 |

| COUNTDOWN | 10 |
| Wedding Calendar | 10 |

| THE ENGAGEMENT | 18 |
| Newspaper Announcements | 18 |
| Choosing Rings | 19 |
| The Engagement Party | 23 |

| WEDDING DECISIONS | 31 |
| Choosing a Date for the Wedding | 31 |
| Finding a New Home | 33 |
| Who Pays for What? | 35 |
| Who Does What? | 36 |
| Colour Schemes | 37 |
| Choosing the Attendants | 38 |
| Wedding Day Clothes | 44 |

| INVITING THE WEDDING GUESTS | 48 |
| How Many? | 48 |
| Ordering Printed Invitations | 50 |
| Stag/Hen Party | 58 |

## ARRANGING THE CEREMONY 60

Choosing Church or Register Office 60
Register Office Marriage Statement 63
Religious Ceremonies 64
  Church of England 64
  Church of Scotland 66
  Irish Weddings 66
  Roman Catholic 67
  Anglo-Catholic 67
  Non-Conformist and Free Churches 67
  Methodist Church 67
  Quaker Weddings 68
  European Christian Weddings 69
  Jewish Weddings 69
  Muslim Weddings 71
  Hindu Hosts and Guests 72
  Sikh Ceremonies 72
  Bahais 72
  Buddhist 73
  Oriental 73
  Mixed-Faith Marriages 73

## TRANSPORT 77

Guests' Arrival 77
Transport To Church/Register Office 77
Transport To Reception 78
Going Away Car 79
Foreign Wedding Customs to Copy 81
Transport Checklist 82

## PLANNING THE WEDDING RECEPTION 84

Where to hold the Reception 84
Professional Catering 84
Drinks 86
Budget Celebration 87

Self-Catering                          87
Receptions Held at Home                88
Seating Plans                          91
Toastmasters                           93
Cake Cutting                           94
Speeches                               95
Photographs                            97
Videotaping                            99
Entertainment                         100
Dancing                               103

## WEDDING GIFTS                      106
Making Wedding Lists                  106
Delivering Gifts at the Wedding       113

## THE HONEYMOON                      116

## HAPPY EVER AFTER                   119

## INDEX                              125

# INTRODUCTION

'It will be all right on the day,' they say, and so it will be if you plan your wedding carefully. This book is designed to give practical at-a-glance information that will take the stress out of planning. Checklists and reminders will help you to have everything ready and to be serenely confident on the day. In addition you will find that the book suggests some good ideas you can copy, those little extra touches which convert a conventional wedding into a special occasion you will remember all your life.

The book is designed to be easy to use. The reason for the order is the time sequence. Read the section on where to hold your wedding ceremony before the section on booking the transport to get you there. In 'Transport' you will find grouped together facts about cars to the church or register office, onward to the reception, and the departure car for the honeymoon. Cross-referencing will enable you to look ahead and co-ordinate the transport. Similarly you are referred from engagement party gifts to wedding gifts, so that you can avoid duplication.

## BEING WELL ORGANIZED

Keep a large, brightly-coloured, easy-to-find hardback record book for written notes, in a permanent place under your desk phone, or in a bedside table drawer cleared of clutter. This prevents you writing on numerous scaps of paper which would create chaos. To prevent other people giving you bits of paper, use a handbag-size notebook to enable you to keep notes together. Friends can write suggestions in that. A duplicate book is useful for distributing copies of addresses to helpers. Duplicate writing pads enable you to keep copies of handwritten letters. Copy important information into your record book each day, having gathered together notes or business cards in a see-through pocket attached to the back of the book with a clip.

Other useful devices for grouping cards or leaflets permanently are:

For business cards: a card index; a loose-leaf indexed business card holder; see-through pages which fix in a Filofax or similar system.

For leaflets: a loose-leaf folder to hold caterers' brochures, letters, and hotel leaflets.

A wedding album with transparent stick-down pages can display the most amusing business cards and pretty sample wedding invitations you wish to show the family. Later it can display your own wedding invitation, printed wedding menu, and favourite congratulations cards.

Throughout your planning, as you make the major decisions you can enter your important names, addresses and telephone numbers in this book.

# COUNTDOWN

A glance at this list will give you a clear idea from the start of what is ahead and will need doing. You can meticulously plan every detail the way you want it. However, if you are short of time you can leave many decisions to the experts who always like to plan happy surprises. The banqueting manager of a large hotel, for example, can arrange for the toastmaster, menu printing, a harpist to play as guests enter, and a band. Good hotels can also be relied upon to deal with minor mishaps – the cloakroom attendant being prepared to sew on a button at the wedding reception, or during your honeymoon.

## WEDDING CALENDAR

### FIRST MONTH AFTER ENGAGEMENT

(First Four To Six Months in Advance)

☆ Tell family

☆ Families meet

☆ Write engagement announcement letters

☆ Buy file or record book of wedding arrangements

☆ Insert engagement announcements in newspaper

☆ Buy engagement and wedding rings

☆ Choose best man, bridesmaids, ushers, pageboys

☆ Hold engagement party

☆ Book church/Meet minister

☆ Collect register office forms

☆ Collect documents to accompany register office forms

☆ Return register office forms

☆ Get caterers' estimates and hotel literature

☆ Meet hotel restaurant banqueting manager

☆ Book caterer, band, toastmaster

☆ Book reception hall or venue

☆ Consult travel agent

☆ Book honeymoon

☆ Order printed invitations, reply cards, serviettes, menus, seating plan

☆ Visit stores to set up wedding lists

☆ Start house hunting by contacting house agents

☆ Contact mortgage brokers and solicitors

☆ Photocopy map of church and reception locations

☆ Appoint solicitor to advise and deal with house exchange and new will

☆ Start making wedding dress if not buying it

☆ Have bridesmaids' dresses made if not buying them

## THREE MONTHS BEFORE WEDDING

☆ Choose wedding cake

☆ Select menu

☆ Choose wedding dress if hiring or buying

☆ Choose bridesmaids' dresses if buying

☆ Attend minister's courses for couples

☆ Thank guests who send presents

☆ Order new passport

☆ See doctor or family planning clinic

## TWO MONTHS BEFORE WEDDING

☆ Send out invitations

☆ Order passports, visas and vaccinations

☆ Mother and mother-in-law choose dresses

☆ Arrange insurance and connection of services at new home

☆ Arrange vaccinations and visas for honeymoon

☆ Visit register office to collect and return forms

## MONTH BEFORE WEDDING

☆ Banns are called in church on three successive Sundays

☆ Select photographer/video company

☆ Book wedding cars

☆ Write speech

☆ Deliver notification to registrar

☆ Choose flowers

☆ Choose music

☆ Get order-of-service sheets printed

☆ Get travellers' cheques

☆ Get insurance for bride to drive groom's car

☆ Select going away outfits

☆ Buy attendants' gifts and wrap them

☆ Make sure groom, best man and ushers have booked hired morning dress

## TWO WEEKS BEFORE WEDDING

☆ Order new address stationery

☆ Take possession of new house

☆ Get phone connected

☆ Deliver furniture and gifts

☆ Book bride's hairdressing appointment

☆ Make seating plan

## WEEK BEFORE WEDDING

☆ Attend wedding rehearsal/Watch another wedding

☆ Notify *The Times* newspaper on Friday for Monday announcement

☆ Collect honeymoon tickets from travel agent

☆ Collect certificates/licence from registrar

☆ Place passports and documents in flight bag/going away handbag

☆ Wear-in new shoes

☆ Confirm all arrangements including cars

☆ Check route to church

☆ Bride's mother checks guests' RSVP cards, phones those who haven't replied, and confirms numbers with caterer

| TWO DAYS BEFORE WEDDING |
| --- |

☆ Families from abroad arrive

☆ Hold stag party/Girls' night out

☆ Guests who cannot attend organize telegrams

| DAY BEFORE WEDDING |
| --- |

☆ Families from distant towns arrive

☆ Bride has hairdressing appointment and manicure

☆ Set-up gift display

☆ Deliver luggage to hotel

☆ Collect buttonholes or wedding cake if necessary

☆ Clean family car and fill it with petrol

☆ Clean and tidy house

☆ Bride's mother notifies caterer of late cancellations/ final guests' numbers

☆ Put clothes ready, speech in pocket

☆ Clean shoes

☆ Set alarm clock

☆ Deliver schedule to minister (Scotland)

## WEDDING DAY

☆ Best man phones groom and ushers to wake them and remedy hitches

☆ Florist delivers bride's bouquet of fresh flowers and bride's mother's corsage to bride's home, other corsages and buttonholes to groom's or best man's home or the church

☆ Best man dresses then arrives at groom's home, places ring and church fees in pockets

☆ Chief bridesmaid arrives at bride's home

☆ Bride has face made up and is dressed in wedding clothes

☆ Professional photographer arrives to photograph bride at home

☆ Flowers are delivered to church and arranged by florist

☆ Ushers arrive at church and show guests to seats

☆ First car takes groom and best man to church

☆ Second car takes bride's mother and bridesmaids to church

☆ Third, grandest, car brings bride and her father to church

## WEDDING CEREMONY

☆ Signing register

☆ Best man pays vicar and church fees

☆ Photographs on church steps

☆ Grandest car takes bride and groom to reception

☆ Second car takes host and other parents of bride/groom

☆ Third car takes bridesmaids and/or ushers

☆ Final car takes best man and any guests lacking transport

☆ More photographs

☆ Receiving line

☆ Drinks

☆ Grace by minister

☆ Buffet or dinner

## CAKE CUTTING

☆ Sparkling wine served for speeches and toasts by bride's father/family/friend, bridegroom, best man

☆ Groom presents bouquet to bride's mother and/or gifts to attendants

☆ Read telegrams

☆ Dancing

☆ Bride and groom change into going away clothes

☆ Decorate departure car

☆ Departure car departs

☆ Bride's father pays and tips caterers

☆ Clear up hall

☆ Best man takes bridesmaids home

## AFTER WEDDING

☆ Return hired wedding clothes

☆ Send of pieces of wedding cake

☆ Thank guests who sent telegrams

☆ Thank guests for presents delivered on wedding day

☆ Select and pay for wedding photographs

# THE ENGAGEMENT

Inform close relatives first by phoning or writing, afterwards friends, then employers and colleagues, including the personnel department, discussing honeymoon dates to avoid the firm's busy period. Finally insert newspaper announcements, which are usually paid for by the bride's family.

## NEWSPAPER ANNOUNCEMENTS

Under Forthcoming Engagements in national newspapers such as *The Times* and *The Daily Telegraph* you can announce an engagement. Phone to get prices and copy deadline dates. The wording is:

Mr J. L. Brown
and Miss A. E. Smith
The engagement is announced between John, son of Mr and Mrs Graham Brown, of London, and Anne, daughter of Mr and Mrs Peter Smith of Glasgow.

Longer announcements cover more detailed relationships if the parents are widowed or divorced. The bride and groom who have several brothers and sisters may wish to indicate that that bride is the 'elder daughter of' her parents, or that the groom is the 'younger son' to avoid confusion.

Announcements can also be made in local newspapers and religious publications. Buy the engagement ring in time to wear it on the day the announcements appear in newspapers.

## CHOOSING RINGS

### BUYING THE ENGAGEMENT RING

Nowadays most couples choose the engagement ring together. The Diamond Information Centre suggests you spend a month's salary on a diamond engagement ring. So that you do not have a harder ring rubbing a softer one, the engagement ring and wedding ring should be the same quality of gold. Matching sets can be bought.

Shop around to compare prices and styles. Illustrated brochures are available from high street jewellers, large suppliers and trade associations such as the National Association of Goldsmiths (Tel. 01–726 4374), London Diamond Centre, or the Diamond Information Centre in London (Tel. 01–404 4444). Individual jewellers make rings to order. When ordering rings by post allow three to four weeks.

★ *GOLD RINGS* The bride's engagement ring is tradition- ally gold with a diamond or other precious stone. Solid gold is used because the ring must be of value. Gold plate can wear off and base metals can make the finger go green when the hand perspires. Gold can be nine carat, eighteen carat or 24 carat. The purest gold is soft and less practical as it can be damaged when striking objects or rubbing other rings, so it is mixed with a harder metal. Nine or eighteen carat gold is preferred for practical reasons and economy. European rings are available in eight carat. An eighteen carat ring is more appropriate for a girl whose other jewellery is eighteen carat gold, as with much Asian jewellery. Although platinum is silver-coloured it is more expensive than gold. It is a very acceptable alternative. Royalty have rings made of Welsh gold: a natural choice for the Princess of Wales.

★ *DIAMONDS* Diamonds are called a girl's best friend because of their value. When choosing a diamond consider the 4 Cs: colour, clarity, cut, and carat (weight). Better (and therefore generally more expensive) diamonds have more sparkle. Diamonds are also chosen because they are durable, go with any colour clothing, and are supposed to bring good luck. The diamond is a symbol of innocence and loyalty, and sacred to the month of April, a popular time for marriages.

★ *CHOOSING A STYLE AND SETTING* Some rings are designed so that extra stones can be added later. If you want a colourful ring, have a central coloured stone encircled by smaller diamonds, or a diamond encircled by coloured stones. You can also have a line of identical stones, a central stone with two stones in contrasting colour of the same size inset in the band, or a raised central stone with two smaller stones in a different colour on the shoulders of the ring.

If you have a second-hand or inherited ring you can alter the ring size and modernize an old ring to make it fashionable. Large stones look impressive twinkling under candle-light. But big flashy rings may snag stockings and hurt your fingers if you knock your hands. Flat styles are practical for everyday wear under gloves. Matching engagement and wedding rings sets are made with interlocking shapes.

## OTHER STONES AND THEIR MEANINGS

Birthstones can be used instead of diamonds, or in addition:

★ *JANUARY* — Garnet (red), for faithfulness

★ *FEBRUARY* — Amethyst (transparent purple) for peace-making

★ *MARCH* — Aquamarine or bloodstone for courage and wisdom

★ *APRIL* — Diamond for innocence or blue sapphire for hope

★ *MAY* — Emerald green for true love

★ *JUNE* — Pearl or agate for health and long life

★ *JULY* — Ruby for friendship or onyx for mutual love

★ *AUGUST* — Peridot (greenish yellow) or sard-onyx (white onyx layers alternating with yellow or orange sard) for a happy marriage

★ *SEPTEMBER* — Sapphire or olive green chrysolite for 'freedom from evil'

★ *OCTOBER* — Opal for hope

★ *NOVEMBER* — Topaz for friendship

★ *DECEMBER* — Turquoise for happiness in love.

### GROOM'S ENGAGEMENT GIFT/WEDDING RING

The girl can buy her fiancé any gift he likes, such as a gold key ring, watch, cuff links, tie pin, silk tie, clothes or a signet ring. His and Hers rings are available in matching styles and can be romantically engraved with names and dates.

### WEDDING RINGS

Gold is produced in various colours – yellow, pink, white, silver, or a combination for toning with other jewellery. A groom's ring can match the bride's. His ring will be pricier because it is larger. Both rings can be engraved with date and name. The groom might prefer a signet ring, or a practical gift such as a watch.

### SAFETY AND INSURANCE OF RINGS

Jewellers supply pretty ring boxes with cushioned linings. When washing your hands return the ring to its protective box within an inside zipped pocket or a securely fastened handbag. If you are not wearing your ring on honeymoon, avoid losing it by securing it, for example, to a necklace, bracelet, or soft watchstrap. Replace the ring before travelling in crowds. Keep the receipt for insurance purposes.

| JEWELLERY SHOP |
| --- |

Name .................................................................................................................

Address ...............................................................................................................

.......................................................................... Tel. ...............................

Goods acceptable/Not acceptable (reason price/quality/

other ........................................... Family informed   No/Yes.

Purchase made by phone No/Yes.   Order in writing

No/Yes.   By (name) .......................................................................

Date .................. To (name) ...............................................................

Written confirmation received   No/Yes (date) ................

from (name) ..........................................................................................

Insurance ............................................................................................

## THE ENGAGEMENT PARTY

Before the engagement party clean the engagement
ring by removing grease with washing-up water and a
toothbrush so that the ring looks its best. It may
continue to be worn with the wedding ring after the
marriage. A manicure ensures that hands look pretty in
photographs.

Pre-printed engagement party invitations can be
bought from stationers. You do not need to organize
any speeches though somebody may choose to make a
toast. For the toast you can provide a sparkling wine,
Bucks Fizz (champagne and orange juice), a champagne
cocktail, or champagne (cider, Coke or mineral water
for children and abstainers). Engagement parties can be
formal seated dinners for the family, with a young
people's party at his or her home.

## GUEST LIST

| GUEST NAME | ADDRESS/ PHONE | INVITED ACCEPTED/ REFUSED |
|---|---|---|
| ★ *WEDDING GROUP* | | |
| His family | | |
| .................................... | .................................... | .................................... |
| .................................... | .................................... | .................................... |
| .................................... | .................................... | .................................... |
| .................................... | .................................... | .................................... |
| .................................... | .................................... | .................................... |
| .................................... | .................................... | .................................... |
| .................................... | .................................... | .................................... |
| .................................... | .................................... | .................................... |
| .................................... | .................................... | .................................... |
| .................................... | .................................... | .................................... |
| .................................... | .................................... | .................................... |
| .................................... | .................................... | .................................... |
| Her family | | |
| .................................... | .................................... | .................................... |
| .................................... | .................................... | .................................... |
| .................................... | .................................... | .................................... |
| .................................... | .................................... | .................................... |
| .................................... | .................................... | .................................... |
| .................................... | .................................... | .................................... |
| .................................... | .................................... | .................................... |
| .................................... | .................................... | .................................... |
| .................................... | .................................... | .................................... |
| .................................... | .................................... | .................................... |
| .................................... | .................................... | .................................... |
| .................................... | .................................... | .................................... |

## GUEST LIST

| HAS TRANSPORT/ ACCOM- MODATION | SENT GIFT | WAS THANKED |
|---|---|---|
| ........................ | ........................ | ........................ |
| ........................ | ........................ | ........................ |
| ........................ | ........................ | ........................ |
| ........................ | ........................ | ........................ |
| ........................ | ........................ | ........................ |
| ........................ | ........................ | ........................ |
| ........................ | ........................ | ........................ |
| ........................ | ........................ | ........................ |
| ........................ | ........................ | ........................ |
| ........................ | ........................ | ........................ |
| ........................ | ........................ | ........................ |
| ........................ | ........................ | ........................ |
| ........................ | ........................ | ........................ |
| ........................ | ........................ | ........................ |
| ........................ | ........................ | ........................ |
| ........................ | ........................ | ........................ |
| ........................ | ........................ | ........................ |
| ........................ | ........................ | ........................ |
| ........................ | ........................ | ........................ |
| ........................ | ........................ | ........................ |
| ........................ | ........................ | ........................ |
| ........................ | ........................ | ........................ |
| ........................ | ........................ | ........................ |
| ........................ | ........................ | ........................ |

| GUEST LIST | | |
|---|---|---|
| **GUEST NAME** | **ADDRESS/ PHONE** | **INVITED ACCEPTED/ REFUSED** |

**His friends**

| | | |
|---|---|---|
| ............................ | ............................ | ............................ |
| ............................ | ............................ | ............................ |
| ............................ | ............................ | ............................ |
| ............................ | ............................ | ............................ |
| ............................ | ............................ | ............................ |

**Her friends**

| | | |
|---|---|---|
| ............................ | ............................ | ............................ |
| ............................ | ............................ | ............................ |
| ............................ | ............................ | ............................ |
| ............................ | ............................ | ............................ |
| ............................ | ............................ | ............................ |

**Colleagues**

| | | |
|---|---|---|
| ............................ | ............................ | ............................ |
| ............................ | ............................ | ............................ |

**Neighbours**

| | | |
|---|---|---|
| ............................ | ............................ | ............................ |
| ............................ | ............................ | ............................ |

**Others**

| | | |
|---|---|---|
| ............................ | ............................ | ............................ |
| ............................ | ............................ | ............................ |
| ............................ | ............................ | ............................ |

## GUEST LIST

| HAS TRANSPORT/ ACCOM- MODATION | SENT GIFT | WAS THANKED |
|---|---|---|
| .......................... | .......................... | .......................... |
| .......................... | .......................... | .......................... |
| .......................... | .......................... | .......................... |
| .......................... | .......................... | .......................... |
| .......................... | .......................... | .......................... |
| .......................... | .......................... | .......................... |
| .......................... | .......................... | .......................... |
| .......................... | .......................... | .......................... |
| .......................... | .......................... | .......................... |
| .......................... | .......................... | .......................... |
| .......................... | .......................... | .......................... |
| .......................... | .......................... | .......................... |
| .......................... | .......................... | .......................... |
| .......................... | .......................... | .......................... |
| .......................... | .......................... | .......................... |
| .......................... | .......................... | .......................... |
| .......................... | .......................... | .......................... |
| .......................... | .......................... | .......................... |
| .......................... | .......................... | .......................... |
| .......................... | .......................... | .......................... |
| .......................... | .......................... | .......................... |

## SEATING

### ★ TOP TABLE

1 ........................................................................................
2 ........................................................................................
3 ........................................................................................
4 ........................................................................................
**Bride-to-be** ........................................................................
**Fiancé** ...............................................................................
1 ........................................................................................
2 ........................................................................................
3 ........................................................................................
4 ........................................................................................

### ★ HER FAMILY TABLE

1 ........................................................................................
2 ........................................................................................
3 ........................................................................................
4 ........................................................................................
5 ........................................................................................
6 ........................................................................................
7 ........................................................................................
8 ........................................................................................
9 ........................................................................................
10 .......................................................................................

### ★ HIS FAMILY TABLE

1 ........................................................................................
2 ........................................................................................
3 ........................................................................................
4 ........................................................................................
5 ........................................................................................
6 ........................................................................................
7 ........................................................................................
8 ........................................................................................
9 ........................................................................................
10 .......................................................................................

## ★ *HER FRIENDS' TABLE*

1 ....................................................................................................
2 ....................................................................................................
3 ....................................................................................................
4 ....................................................................................................
5 ....................................................................................................
6 ....................................................................................................
7 ....................................................................................................
8 ....................................................................................................
9 ....................................................................................................
10 ...................................................................................................

## ★ *HIS FRIENDS' TABLE*

1 ....................................................................................................
2 ....................................................................................................
3 ....................................................................................................
4 ....................................................................................................
5 ....................................................................................................
6 ....................................................................................................
7 ....................................................................................................
8 ....................................................................................................
9 ....................................................................................................
10 ...................................................................................................

### ENGAGEMENT GIFTS

If you are holding a large party you may be asked what gifts you would like. A wedding gift list can be used for both the engagement party and the wedding reception. (See **Wedding Gifts**.)

### GIFT SHOPS

Local gift shop name .........................................................................

Address ...............................................................................................

................................................................. Tel. ............................

Department store name ................................................

Address ................................................................................

............................................................ Tel. ..........................

Department ..........................................................................

---

| GIFT CHECKLIST |

For which room/type of article/colour/size/brand/price/
still on order/held by store/delivered to new home/
insured/exchanged for.

Donor's name ......................................................................

Address ................................................................................

............................................................ Tel. ..........................

Donor's gift safe arrival acknowledged verbally    No/Yes
Thanked in writing    No/Yes.


For which room/type of article/colour/size/brand/price/
still on order/held by store/delivered to new home/
insured/exchanged for.

Donor's name ......................................................................

Address ................................................................................

............................................................ Tel. ..........................

Donor's gift safe arrival acknowledged verbally    No/Yes
Thanked in writing    No/Yes.

# WEDDING DECISIONS

The best time of year for a wedding depends on the length of your engagement, when you can get time off work, and seasonal weather here and for honeymoons abroad. Check when you can obtain a booking at the church, reception venue, and honeymoon destination, and take possession of your new home. Commitments such as examinations taken by the best man or bridesmaids, or sister-in-law's pregnancies, should also be considered.

### MARRIAGE SEASON

Late spring was previously popular for weddings because there were tax advantages. The weather should not be too cold, long light days are pleasant for bride and groom to travel abroad, and you can pay low- or mid-season prices for the honeymoon.

### SUMMER WEDDINGS

Summer is also popular, allowing guests from abroad or far away to combine the wedding with a summer holiday. Resort hotels are busiest in summer and country hotels tend to be booked for weddings on Saturdays. But many city hotels are less full because business people are away on holiday and conferences which normally fill city hotels are held in autumn and winter. This applies to London, certain inland UK cities, Paris, and New York.

## AUTUMN AND WINTER WEDDINGS

July to September is another popular time for weddings. If you get engaged in the spring and take three to six months to organize the wedding you can marry in late summer, without waiting a whole year for a spring wedding. If one of you is a teacher you might honeymoon in the autumn half-term, when the weather is still reasonable.

Late winter weddings are not ideal for big church weddings because on colder days guests might be delayed by bad weather. The bride and bridesmaids need coats, and you are less sure of getting sunshine for photographs. However, winter is a good time for small weddings in register offices, or marrying abroad, with a skiing honeymoon. Winter honeymoons in the sun are superb if you can afford exotic honeymoon destinations.

## STUDENT MARRIAGES

If you get engaged while studying, time your wedding for after the examinations. Weddings require organization which should not coincide with revision. Marrying while studying does not necessarily interfere with studies. One survey showed that married students did better in examinations because single students looking for a date were expending more time on social life! If you do not want to delay the wedding until studies finish, consider switching to evening study courses.

**Exam dates** ........................................................................................

........................................................................................................

........................................................................................................

## WEEKDAY VERSUS WEEKEND WEDDINGS

Register office weddings take place from Monday to Friday and on Saturday mornings. You can marry in church on Saturday, but not Sunday because that would interfere with church services. Avoid religious festivals, processions, and events such as football matches which result in traffic jams.

Forthcoming events ...................................................................

.....................................................................................................

.....................................................................................................

.....................................................................................................

.....................................................................................................

.....................................................................................................

.....................................................................................................

On weekdays it is easier and cheaper to book reception halls and honeymoon hotels. However, at weekends most guests can get off work more easily. The day of the wedding might also be influenced by the departure day of the honeymoon package tour.

Honeymoon departure day ...............................................

## FINDING A NEW HOME

First agree the location of the new home in city, suburb or country. Proximity to work is one factor. Finance and mortgage are others. If you both work in the city and rely on public transport, draw a line around your two work locations. Where they overlap identify railway stations or bus routes. Pick the good or cheap areas. Then start house hunting using estate agents or newspapers in that area. You may also want to stay near where you live now, or move near parents.

## ★ HOUSE AGENTS

Name ..................................................................................

Address ..............................................................................

........................................................ Tel. ........................

Property to see: Address .....................................................

........................................................ Tel. ........................

Family informed No/Yes. Appointment made by phone

No/Yes. Offer made No/Yes. By (name) ......................

........................................................ Date ......................

To (name) ...................... Written acceptance received

No/Yes (date) ............... from (name) ........................

..................................................................................

Deposit date ............ Contract exchange date ...............

Surveyor name ..................................................................

Address ..............................................................................

........................................................ Tel. ........................

Building Society name .......................................................

Address ..............................................................................

........................................................ Tel. ........................

Mortgage ...........................................................................

Insurance Company name ..................................................

Address ..............................................................................

........................................................ Tel. ........................

Premium paid for building/contents ....................................

From date ......................... Renewal due ...............................

Long engagements can be spent redecorating a property 'needing improvement'. Rebuilding, rewiring, plumbing, glazing and decorating are time-consuming. If the new home is near the register office of church you can hold the wedding reception there, and spend the first night of the honeymoon in it. Ensure the new home is ready before the wedding. If time is running out invite attendants to a painting party, supplying paint and brushes, cassette music, sandwiches and soft drinks.

## WHO PAYS FOR WHAT?

Traditionally the bride's family pays for the wedding and does most of the planning. As a result the bride's family's church is often chosen for the ceremony, and the bride's mother arranges the church flowers. For a first marriage they pay for the wedding reception, the bride's dress and trousseau, and the car from her home to church.

☆ The groom chooses his best man and ushers, and traditionally he and/or his parents pay for: transporting the groom and best man to church, the church service, best man's and ushers' matching accessories (ties and matching pocket handkerchiefs, gloves), buttonholes for the best man, ushers, fathers of bride and groom, the bride's bouquet, church flowers, corsages or flowers for bride's mother's corsage, groom's mother's corsage, the car from the church to the reception, the departure car, the honeymoon, and the home the bridal couple move into.

☆ The best man and ushers buy or hire their own clothes.

## WHO DOES WHAT?

☆ The bride's mother organizes.

☆ The bridesmaids help arrange the bride's clothes and trousseau, and the wedding reception catering.

☆ The bride chooses her dress and her bridesmaids' dresses. Older brides who are already 'wearing the trousers' can organize everything – even a surprise spring wedding at a register office. A well-organized bride timed a wedding before her farming boyfriend got busy with the lambing season, and booked a honeymoon cottage near where they worked.

☆ The bride's father merely pays (after saying how much he is prepared to pay), walks the bride up the aisle, and often gives a speech.

☆ Older couples often share the planning, especially for a second marriage.

☆ The groom's family frequently contributes towards the wedding reception, splitting the bill, or paying for the drinks or the band.

☆ The groom still usually organizes the men, including the priest, transport of himself, best man, and ushers to the church and everybody from the church, chauffeurs, and the honeymoon.

## COLOUR SCHEMES

As the bride, you will be the centre of attention so select dress colours to complement your complexion. Accessories should match your hair and eyes or contrast with your dress. When planning the flowers and dresses, pick a predominant colour or two contrasting colours. Old favourites are pink or baby blue and white. Pastel pink and silver is pretty; deep Italian pink with black is sophisticated.

Everything starts to fall into place once you have chosen a colour scheme and wedding theme. For example, for a spring wedding my bouquet was yellow and white with green leaves, my colour scheme following that decision. If your theme is yellow flowers, plant daffodils in windowboxes for a spring wedding, or yellow roses for a summer wedding reception in your garden. Order the bride a yellow bouquet and hair ribbons, and buy bridesmaids yellow dresses, belts or sashes. Yellow roses decorating the wedding cake can be co-ordinated with yellow serviettes. For a yellow kitchen in the new home put yellow crockery on the wedding present list.

## WHO PAYS FOR CLOTHES?

The father of the bride used to pay for everything, but nowadays usually everyone buys their own clothes in materials and styles they can wear again. But if the bride asks the bridesmaids to wear identical outfits in her colour scheme and a style they cannot wear again, the bride's family may pay. The bride's father still pays if he can more easily afford the clothes, and does not have to finance so many that the cost exceeds his budget. If the bride's younger sister is the only bridesmaid this solves the problem! An older potential bridesmaid who cannot agree with the other older bridesmaid about clothes might be appointed as witness instead.

The groom who asks his best man and ushers to wear dark suits or morning suits in the conventional colours of black or grey with black bow ties or silver cravats can expect the attendants to either already have or need to hire the outfits. But if he imposes an unusual colour scheme for accessories, say red silk ties and matching handkerchiefs, he buys the matching sets which the attendants keep.

## CHOOSING THE ATTENDANTS

The hosts who are paying decide whether to hold a big or small wedding. A first-time bride marrying in a church often likes to have bridesmaids, especially if she has younger sisters, or nieces. The bridesmaid, chief bridesmaid, or maid of honour assists the bride.

### CHIEF BRIDESMAID'S RESPONSIBILITIES

If there are several bridesmaids, some of whom are very young, the oldest may be appointed chief brides-maid. A bride expects more help from a chief bridesmaid who is a sister living in the same house, a flatmate, or the matron-of-honour for an older bride who has no mother. The chief bridesmaid helps the bride dress, looks after younger bridesmaids or page-boys, and stands behind the bride in church holding the bouquet or prayerbook.

Other responsibilities of the chief bridesmaid:

☆ Witness the signatures. Hand the bouquet back to the bride.

☆ Arrange the bride's train for smaller bridesmaids to carry.

☆ Follow the bride in the recession on the arm of the best man.

☆ Pose for photographs.

☆ Act as general assistant at the wedding reception, as hostess or waitress when required.

☆ Carry lipstick and comb for the bride and help her unzip her dress or manage her train when visiting bathroom and changing room.

☆ Catch the bride's bouquet.

☆ Help the bride change into her going away outfit.

☆ Acknowledge the safe arrival of gifts while the bride is away on honeymoon.

## MAID-OF-HONOUR

At a register office wedding where the bride does not wear a long white dress and there are no bridesmaids in frilly dresses, a maid-of-honour may be appointed as companion, wearing a smart suit and similar corsage to the bride.

## MATRON-OF-HONOUR

The matron, i.e. married woman, might be the bride's older married sister. An older woman such as a widow is likely to have a married woman friend as assistant and attendant.

Bridesmaid's name ........................................................................

Address ........................................................................

........................................................ Tel. ........................

## THE BEST MAN

A bridesmaid is not necessary but a best man is. The groom's obvious choice is a brother. Failing that, pick a good friend. If the best man is expected to help the groom organize a large wedding, somebody living nearby is an asset. You can have a best woman, except that it is more awkward for her to help the groom and ushers with their clothes. An older person will be experience, well-organized, and confident. The best man could even be the groom's father.

## THE BEST MAN'S RESPONSIBILITIES

According to the size of the wedding, the initiative of the groom, and other members of the wedding party, the best man does some or all of the following:

☆ Helps select ushers and instructs them on clothing required and church seating plan.

☆ Agrees on clothes style, buys own, or visits hire company with groom and ushers for fitting.

☆ Meets chief bridesmaid/maid-/matron-of-honour to arrange co-ordination.

☆ Writes speech.

☆ Organizes stag party venue, transport, food and drink.

☆ Checks route to church.

☆ Attends church rehearsal.

☆ On the day phones and wakes the groom. Phones and wakes ushers.

☆ Dresses in wedding clothes. Puts speech notes in pocket.

☆ Travels to groom's house. Collects from groom the ring, church fees, and travel documents.

☆ Helps groom dress.

☆ Phones car hire company to confirm they are coming or checks that car starts.

☆ Gets groom to church on time.

☆ Looks after wedding ring and hands it over at marriage ceremony.

☆ Handles licences or documents required for wedding.

☆ Makes payment of church fees.

☆ Acts as witness signing register.

☆ Escorts chief bridesmaid in recession.

☆ With aid of ushers gets guests onto church steps for group photograph.

☆ Stands in group photograph on church steps. Then ushers bride and groom into first car.

☆ Arranges transport of entire wedding party, groom and bride, bride's and groom's parents, bridesmaids, and stray guests, from church or register office to reception.

☆ Acts as toastmaster, announcing guests at receiving line at reception.

☆ Announces that minister or bride's father will say grace.

☆ Calls for silence for the cake cutting.

☆ Delivers speech. Reads telegrams. Keeps the telegrams and gives them to the bride's mother after reading them, at the end of the evening, or next day.

☆ Announces first dance and last dance, if any. Dances with bride, bridesmaids.

☆ Looks after groom's accessories such as top hat, and luggage.

☆ Helps groom change into departure clothes while ushers decorate departure car, or, together with the ushers and friends, decorates departure car while groom is changing.

☆ Keeps travel documents and hands them over to groom − or bride.

☆ Drives couple to departure point and returns car and hired wedding clothes.

☆ Supervises clearing of reception hall, collecting lost property.

☆ Sees that bridesmaids and stray guests get home safely.

☆ Returns own and groom's hire clothes to hire company, collecting deposits.

☆ Buys spare copies of local paper containing wedding pictures.

More details can be found in *How To Be The Best Man* by Angela Lansbury, published in this series.

Best man's name ..................................................................................................

Address ...............................................................................................................

.............................................................................. Tel. ...............................

## USHERS' RESPONSIBILITIES

A general rule is one usher for every fifty guests, up to four ushers. Ushers will:

☆ Meet groom and best man to agree on clothing.

☆ Visit hire company for fitting.

☆ Buy clothing accessories, or collect tie and handkerchief from groom or best man.

☆ Be guests at stag party.

☆ Be first to arrive in church. Collect buttonhole flowers from florist decorating church.

☆ See that car park attendant has removed barrier. Or appoint one usher to stay at entrance to car park, directing guests, turning away or redirecting lost passers-by.

☆ Greet guests arriving in church.

☆ Hand out order-of-service sheets.

☆ Ask guests whether they are friends of 'the bride or the groom'.

☆ Direct guests to seats, bride's family and friends on the left of the altar, the groom's on the right.

☆ Walk VIPs to their seats, i.e. groom's parents, bride's mother. One usher should be delegated to wait and escort the bride's mother, giving her his arm, preferably the chief usher who is her oldest son. But if he is best man, her second son is the choice.

☆ After the bride enters, close the church door.

☆ As bridal party sets off down aisle for recession, open church door.

☆ Organize one usher to go to house where reception is being held to direct parking.

☆ Hand out drinks.

☆ Be photographed with groom and best man.

☆ Pay compliments to bridesmaids and dance with them if they do not have other escorts.

☆ Escort bridesmaids, grannies and other stray guests home.

Usher's name ..........................................................................................

Address ..................................................................................................

.................................................................... Tel. ................................

## WEDDING DAY CLOTHES

### BRIDE'S WEDDING CLOTHES

Traditional wedding gowns in white or cream can be bought or rented from bridal shops, obtained second-hand, or made to order. The dress with a long train has no purpose after the wedding but can be stored or sold. A suntan looks good with a white dress. Dresses and hats can be hired.

### BRIDE'S ACCESSORIES

The head-dress might be a circlet or Juliet cap, tiara, or silk flowers. Also buy a veil, hat, hair ribbons or pretty hairclips, taking into account the bride's hairstyle. The hairdresser may be able to plan an unusual style such as white ribbons forming a lattice in dark hair, or ribbons woven into braids. The bride's shoes could be leather or satin pumps dyed to match accessories.

The bride is supposed to wear or carry Something Old (representing sentiment and constancy) which could be a watch; Something New (for a new start) which could be the wedding dress or veil; Something

Borrowed (symbolizing friendship), which could be a handkerchief, brooch, or bracelet; and Something Blue (for luck) which could be a garter, panties, flowers, a hair ribbon, small blue bow on underclothes, belt on sash, watchface, or jewel.

## THE BRIDE'S BOUQUET

Although the groom pays, the bride chooses the flowers. Her bouquet could be all white, or contrasting colours such as pink and lavender, or several shades of one colour such as salmon pink.

## BRIDE'S GOING AWAY OUTFIT

For travelling to the honeymoon destination most brides change into a smart suit and hat with new bag and shoes, or a pretty summer dress. After the wedding you can sell the wedding dress or preserve it to wear on an anniversary or give to a daughter.

## GROOM, BEST MAN AND USHERS

In addition to the lounge suit, dinner jacket, or morning suit and hat, the men require a dressy shirt and tie. Group fittings can be arranged at hire shops. Hiring black or grey suits is cheaper than buying and ensures the outfits are in current fashion. (Larger hire shops have blue and brown suits.) An outfit of suit, shirt and tie/cravat is available at under £50 for three days' hire (borrow the day before, return the day after). White gloves and cuff links with black onyx are obtainable from menswear hire shops. Co-ordinating sets of accessories such as silk ties and matching handkerchiefs can be bought. Watch straps should be suitably smart. Socks should co-ordinate with shoes. Black the base of shoes as they will be visible when kneeling at the church altar. Buttonholes are generally carnations, fresh flowers being preferred though fabric flowers are available. Florists can advise on seasonal flowers and colours.

## BRIDESMAIDS' OUTFITS

Dresses should be in the same colour but may be in varying styles according to the bridesmaids' ages. Accessories which should co-ordinate include gloves, parasols, shoes, tights, hairbands, and cosmetics. The bridesmaids' posies might include silver leaves and some lavender to provide scent. Their headbands could have matching flowers.

## MOTHER AND MOTHER-IN-LAW

They can choose their own colours, after the bride and bridesmaids have selected theirs, so that styles and colours such as reds and oranges and pinks do not clash. The mother and mother-in-law should co-ordinate styles and colours and not wear black (too funereal) or white (confusing or distracting attention from the bride).

## PAGEBOYS' OUTFITS

Popular pageboys' outfits are velvet pageboy suits with a velvet jacket and matching velvet cut-off trousers, or a three-piece suit. Colours available include navy, aubergine, black, brown or silver-grey. To complete the outfit the boys can wear white dress shirts and dark bow ties plus black patent shoes with silver buckles. Alternatively, a pageboy could be teamed with a little bridesmaid and wear a cream shirt with lacy jabot (central frill), cream moiré pantaloons, and cummerbund in colours echoing her sash. Other possibilities are a wool knit, a sailor suit, or a Guardsman's uniform. These are available by mail order from London.

## ★ *CLOTHES HIRE SHOP*

Name ...........................................................................................

Address .......................................................................................

.......................................................................................................

........................................................... Tel. ...............................

Prices: Deposit ............................... Hire ..............................

Extras .........................................................................................

.......................................................................................................

Penalty for late return ........................................Acceptable/

Not acceptable (reason/price/quality/availability/

other ............................................................................. ).

Family informed No/Yes. Appointment made by

phone No/Yes. Hire agreement in writing No/Yes.

By (name) .................................................................................

........................................................... Date ...............................

To (name) .................................................................................

Written confirmation received No/Yes (date) ...........

From (name) .............................................................................

Collection date .........................................................................

Name of person collecting clothes ...............................

Name of person returning clothes ...............................

Return date ...............................................................................

Deposit reclaimed by (name) ...........................................

Deposit returned to groom (name) ...............................

# INVITING THE
# WEDDING GUESTS

## HOW MANY?

List all those people you would both like to invite: relatives, friends, schoolfriends, workmates, people you know from social clubs, neighbours, and those who invited you to their wedding. Your address book is the first prompter. If you held a large engagement party you may want to refer back to your previous guest list (though you may then need to pare the numbers down to keep within your budget).

## COSTS

Discuss with whoever is paying the maximum number they envisage entertaining. The bride's father might be willing to tell his daughter the limit of the budget. Decide whether you would prefer to have a smaller number of guests at the ideal venue enjoying an extensive menu, or more guests at a less glossy location. Greater numbers mean higher costs. For costly weddings you may have to leave a deposit, and insure against cancellation, which would involve loss of the catering deposit.

| SAMPLE COSTS |
| --- |

★ *TWENTY GUESTS* Food at £5 per head would cost £100, food costing £10 per head = £200, food at £20 per head = £400.

★ *FIFTY GUESTS* Food at £5 per head = £250, at £10 per head = £500, at £20 per head = £1,000.

★ *ONE HUNDRED GUESTS* Food at £5 per head = £500, food at £10 per head = £1,000, food at £20 per head = £2,000.

★ *MORE THAN ONE HUNDRED GUESTS* A £10 meal for two hundred means £2,000, for three hundred, £3,000, and so on.

As numbers of guests increase, allow for a proportionally extra cost for a larger wedding cake, more drinks, service, VAT, hire of hall, toastmaster, entertainer or band, flowers, balloons and favours.

## CHILDREN

You might exclude children because you must limit numbers, or because the celebration will continue until late at night. If the problem is cost, you might exclude teenagers from a dinner, but invite them to come along later for the dancing.

## EQUAL NUMBERS OF RELATIVES FROM EACH SIDE

The host should allow for the groom's family to require an equal number of guests. If the groom's family is larger, a compromise might be reached if the groom's family want to contribute to the cost, providing that the bride's family don't mind being outnumbered.

## ADDITIONS AND DELETIONS

You will probably find that a few extra people have to be invited. Somebody gets engaged or married and cannot come without their partner. You realize that you have forgotten to include the minister and his wife. You have not listed yourself or the immediate wedding party. The family in Canada who you thought would not come have arranged their holiday specially to make it possible.

If your numbers are large the extras may be balanced out by a few late cancellations. Guests are too sick with colds or flu or too pregnant to travel distances. They are abroad because of work or holidays. They suffer minor mishaps like pulled muscles, broken limbs or lost teeth.

Number of party guests ...........................................................................

Number of guests at seated dinner ...........................................................

Number of children ...............................................................................

Number to arrive after dinner ................................................................

Numbers at separate disco/other party ....................................................

## ORDERING PRINTED INVITATIONS

High street stationers have books of sample invitations showing wording and printing styles on different quality paper and card. For a large formal wedding engraving on thick card with silver or gold edges is appropriate. The same printer can usually print order-of-service sheets, and menus with a list of toasts. You can also order placecards and printed items such as matchbooks and balloons.

## TYPICAL WORDINGS

Mr and Mrs John Brown request the pleasure of the company of ...........................................................................
at a reception to celebrate the marriage of their daughter Anne Marie to Mr Michael Hastings at ......................................................................................................
on ......................................................................................................

The widowed mother who has remarried and is acting host with her second husband informs you that:

Mr and Mrs Peter Green ...... to the marriage of her daughter ......

The bride and groom, acting hosts:

Miss Anne Marie Brown and Mr Michael Hastings request the pleasure of your company at a reception to celebrate their marriage ......

or

The pleasure of the company of ...... is requested at the marriage of Miss Anne Marie Brown to Mr Michael Hastings.

or

Anne Marie Brown and Michael Hastings request ......

## SECOND MARRIAGE

If the bride is divorced or widowed she is usually paying for her own wedding without assistance from her father. She keeps her prefix Mrs (especially if she has children), and could use her married surname. Her invitation might read: 'Mrs Anne Matthews invites you to a reception to celebrate . . ' or more usually 'Mr David Brown and Mrs Anne Matthews . . .'.

The invitation goes out before the marriage and reception so if the bride-to-be is widowed she is still Mrs John Brown. (This tells guests who her child Jimmy Brown belongs to.) She may change her name after the marriage.

## OTHER STATIONERY

☆ Order-of-service folded card with words on the cover: Wedding Service/The Wedding Service/Our wedding service.

☆ Placecards for tables: Anne and Stephen, January 26th, 1990.

☆ Serviettes: Thank you for sharing our happiness/joy; Thank you for being with us today and for all your good wishes.

☆ Balloons, matchbooks, cards for wedding cake sent to those who cannot attend: With the compliments of Jane and Steven, January 26th, 1990.

Cards can be printed in silver or gold, with borders of bells or bell-shaped flowers, or cut with oval holes or hearts projecting above the top edge, and matching white envelopes lined with shiny gold paper.

Stationer's/Printer's name .................................................................

Address .................................................................................................

..................................................................... Tel. ................

Acceptable/Not acceptable (reason ..........................................

...................... ).  Family informed  No/Yes.  Order made by phone  No/Yes.  Confirmed in writing  No/Yes. By (name) ...............................................................................

Date .............. To (name) ..................................................

Written confirmation received   No/Yes (date) ...............

From (name) .............................. Deposit ...............

Paid for ............................................... Delivered ...........

## ARRANGING ACCOMMODATION FOR GUESTS

Send hotel lists or brochures to guests who might be staying overnight. The bride's mother can make bookings for guests who live far away. Block bookings in hotels may qualify for a discount, or a free room. If the reception is held in a hotel guests may wish to stay there. Talk to family about accommodation in their homes for close relatives and guests who are on a budget, especially if no reasonable commercial accommodation is nearby.

Arrange to meet VIP relatives at airport or railway station. If you live in a remote country area, tell guests which train to catch and send a car, minicab or coach to meet it. A small van can run a shuttle service.

Local hotel name .................................................

Address ..............................................................

..............................................................

.................................... Reservation tel. ...............

Local car hire company name .........................

Address ..............................................................

.................................... Tel. ...............

Price station to home .........................................

Price station to hotel .........................................

## GUEST LIST

| GUEST NAME | ADDRESS/ PHONE | INVITED ACCEPTED/ REFUSED |
|---|---|---|
| ★ *WEDDING GROUP* | | |
| His family | | |
| .................................. | .................................. | .................................. |
| .................................. | .................................. | .................................. |
| .................................. | .................................. | .................................. |
| .................................. | .................................. | .................................. |
| .................................. | .................................. | .................................. |
| .................................. | .................................. | .................................. |
| .................................. | .................................. | .................................. |
| .................................. | .................................. | .................................. |
| .................................. | .................................. | .................................. |
| .................................. | .................................. | .................................. |
| .................................. | .................................. | .................................. |
| .................................. | .................................. | .................................. |
| Her family | | |
| .................................. | .................................. | .................................. |
| .................................. | .................................. | .................................. |
| .................................. | .................................. | .................................. |
| .................................. | .................................. | .................................. |
| .................................. | .................................. | .................................. |
| .................................. | .................................. | .................................. |
| .................................. | .................................. | .................................. |
| .................................. | .................................. | .................................. |
| .................................. | .................................. | .................................. |
| .................................. | .................................. | .................................. |
| .................................. | .................................. | .................................. |
| .................................. | .................................. | .................................. |
| .................................. | .................................. | .................................. |

| GUEST LIST | | |
|---|---|---|
| **HAS TRANSPORT/ ACCOM- MODATION** | **SENT GIFT** | **WAS THANKED** |
| | | |
| | | |
| | | |
| | | |
| | | |
| | | |
| | | |
| | | |
| | | |
| | | |
| | | |
| | | |
| | | |
| | | |
| | | |
| | | |
| | | |
| | | |
| | | |
| | | |
| | | |
| | | |
| | | |
| | | |
| | | |
| | | |
| | | |
| | | |

## GUEST LIST

| GUEST NAME | ADDRESS/ PHONE | INVITED ACCEPTED/ REFUSED |
| --- | --- | --- |
| **His friends** | | |
| .................... | .................... | .................... |
| .................... | .................... | .................... |
| .................... | .................... | .................... |
| .................... | .................... | .................... |
| .................... | .................... | .................... |
| .................... | .................... | .................... |
| **Her friends** | | |
| .................... | .................... | .................... |
| .................... | .................... | .................... |
| .................... | .................... | .................... |
| .................... | .................... | .................... |
| .................... | .................... | .................... |
| .................... | .................... | .................... |
| **Colleagues** | | |
| .................... | .................... | .................... |
| .................... | .................... | .................... |
| .................... | .................... | .................... |
| **Neighbours** | | |
| .................... | .................... | .................... |
| .................... | .................... | .................... |
| .................... | .................... | .................... |
| **Others** | | |
| .................... | .................... | .................... |
| .................... | .................... | .................... |
| .................... | .................... | .................... |
| .................... | .................... | .................... |

## GUEST LIST

| HAS TRANSPORT/ ACCOM- MODATION | SENT GIFT | WAS THANKED |
| --- | --- | --- |
| .................................... | .................................... | .................................... |
| .................................... | .................................... | .................................... |
| .................................... | .................................... | .................................... |
| .................................... | .................................... | .................................... |
| .................................... | .................................... | .................................... |
| .................................... | .................................... | .................................... |
| .................................... | .................................... | .................................... |
| .................................... | .................................... | .................................... |
| .................................... | .................................... | .................................... |
| .................................... | .................................... | .................................... |
| .................................... | .................................... | .................................... |
| .................................... | .................................... | .................................... |
| .................................... | .................................... | .................................... |
| .................................... | .................................... | .................................... |
| .................................... | .................................... | .................................... |
| .................................... | .................................... | .................................... |
| .................................... | .................................... | .................................... |
| .................................... | .................................... | .................................... |
| .................................... | .................................... | .................................... |
| .................................... | .................................... | .................................... |

# STAG/HEN PARTY

A good time for a stag party is a week before the wedding, perhaps the evening of the wedding rehearsal when the attendants are gathered together and the wedding seems imminent. If the stag party requires the presence of guests coming from abroad it may have to be held two nights before the wedding. The best man arranges it.

## STAG/HEN PARTY VENUES

Many publicans dislike hiring rooms to single-sex groups watching a stripper as it spoils the family atmosphere for other customers. The publican could also lose his licence for keeping a disorderly house. He is bound by law not to serve anyone who appears to be intoxicated and is empowered to exclude anyone without giving a reason. If anyone refuses to leave he can call the police. So if you are asked to leave a pub do not argue.

If there is any trouble at a stag party the best man should apologize to the publican and bystanders, ensure that all the drinks are paid for, that any damage is recompensed, and transport everyone home safely.

One solution is to have the men and women separate in adjoining rooms and all meet together later.

## STAG/HEN PARTY ENTERTAINMENT – SPOOF SPEECHES

Props for funny photographs and speeches can be obtained from fancy dress shops, toyshops, or improvised, e.g. plastic handcuffs, a ball and chain, apron as gift to the bride-to-be and matching chef's apron for the groom with extra long apron strings, plus pinboard or message pad inscribed 'Your dinner is in the dog'.

The best man can assure the groom that he has written a wedding speech, and play Rowan Atkinson's humorous speech or write a similar disaster speech. You could also improvise a spoof radio programme in advance, asking the bride and passers-by, 'Do you know John Smith (groom's name)? Is he the most eligible bachelor in this city? Should a handsome man of his age get married?' Play it back at the stag party. Alternatively, do this live in the pub at the stag party. Censor the boys' tape which can be played at the girls' hen party. The bridesmaids can make a similar tape for the boys.

## TRANSPORT HOME

Organize transport home at a reasonable hour, preventing groom and guests getting too tiddly. Apart from major disasters, like injuries, court cases, or losing your driver's licence, you risk minor mishaps like denting the wedding car, or waking up late next day!

The girls could hold their hen party at the bride's home and drink soft drinks or coffee and turn up dressed as parking wardens or prison officers to drive the boys home.

## STAG/HEN FANCY DRESS PARTIES AT HOME

You can hold an amusing stag/hen party at the groom's house. The best man, a hired actor, or the bride, can dress as a butler to welcome guests. Or the best man could dress as a waitress in drag (borrowing a wig in the bride-to-be's hair colour). Order guests to wipe their feet on the doormat, and give a speech about every man needing a woman to look after him. Later the bridesmaids arrive dressed as the girls from St Trinian's. Raid your attic or the local jumble sales for discarded school uniforms. Don't forget the camera!

The groom is safe at home. Any inebriated guests can snooze on the sofa until sober. (See also personal music under Wedding Music.) (More suggestions are given in *How To Be The Best Man*, companion book to this by the same author, published by Ward Lock.)

# ARRANGING THE CEREMONY

You have banns (verbal public announcements) in the Church of England/Wales of your intention to marry; then after at least three weeks' delay marry according to the rites of the Church of England or Wales, making your vows (verbal statement of agreement to marry) in church and signing the register.

Alternatively give written notification to a register office; after the required days of delay marry in a register office alone, making your statement before the registrar and signing the register in the register office. (You can later go to a religious building for a religious ceremony of blessing.)

You can also get authorization from a register office and then marry in a religious building (such as a synagogue or Quaker Meeting House) which has an appointed registrar and make your statement before him and sign the register there.

## CHOOSING CHURCH OR REGISTER OFFICE

Marriage in the register office alone may be the only option for a second marriage or partners of mixed religion. A register office wedding is less expensive because you need not pay for music, nor elaborate clothes. For the civil marriage you must provide documentary evidence of any divorce.

## MARRIAGE AFTER CIVIL PRELIMINARIES

Notify the superintendent registrar or registrar that you intend to marry and decide whether to marry by certificate or certificate and licence.

## MARRIAGE BY CERTIFICATE

Each of the people intending to marry must notify the superintendent registrar in the district where he/she has been living for a minimum of seven days beforehand. If you both live in the same district you only need to give one notice. The notice is displayed in the register office for 21 days in case there is anyone who knows any reason why you should not marry. Assuming all goes well and the superintendent does not discover any hitches (such as your partner's divorce obtained abroad not being recognized under English law) at the end of the time you get your certificate. This system is the quickest if you are in a hurry. Alternatively obtain a certificate and licence.

## MARRIAGE BY CERTIFICATE AND LICENCE

You only need one notice and either party can give it but you must have been living in the superintendent's district for 15 days before giving notice. It is not displayed. One clear working day must elapse after that (not a Sunday, Good Friday or Christmas Day) and then on the following day (usually the third day), assuming that the superintendent has not found anything wrong, you get the certificate and licence.

## OTHER DETAILS OF PROCEDURE

Full details of procedure for marriages in England and

Wales can be obtained from your local Register Office. Or write to General Register Office, St Catherine's House, 10 Kingsway, London WC2B 6JP, tel. 01–242 0262. Their literature covers most things you might think of asking, plus a few more you never thought of. For example, it tells you what to do if you are marrying abroad because you are in the family of a serviceman stationed overseas or want to legitimize a child born before you got married.

## WHO CAN MARRY WHOM?

Her Majesty's Stationery Office prints leaflets detailing the rules and these are available from your nearest Registrar of Births, Marriages and Deaths. In England the minimum age for marriage is eighteen, sixteen with parental consent. Rules in Scotland are different. Write to your nearest Scottish Register Office for details.

When marrying a foreigner you need documentary confirmation that your marriage would not be illegal in their home country.

For a special licence to marry outside your Anglican parish (because you have sentimental attachment to another church, or have recently arrived from abroad) apply to the Archbishop's Registrar at Lambeth Palace, London.

## SECOND MARRIAGE

Separation over an extended period is sufficient grounds for divorce. The Decree Nisi means you can marry, but not yet. Decree is Latin for thing decided, Nisi is Latin for unless, e.g. unless the divorcees get back together, a divorce decision pending for six weeks, like marriage banns in reverse. Assuming no reason for cancelling it occurs, when you have a Decree Absolute you can go ahead and remarry.

# REGISTER OFFICE MARRIAGE STATEMENT

In a register office the groom speaks first, repeating after the superintendent registrar, 'I do solemnly declare that I know not of any lawful impediment why I (groom's name) may not be joined in matrimony to (bride's name)'. Then the bride makes a similar statement. Afterwards the registrar says the words which the groom repeats, 'I call upon these persons here present to witness that I (groom's name) do take thee (bride's name) to be my lawful wedded wife.' The bride says the same thing. The superintendent says, 'You are now man and wife together'. The wording is prescribed by law.

The wording in a register office for the declaration and contract is standard but may be said in English or Welsh. The two witnesses must be aged over 18. The register office procedure only takes about five to ten minutes.

The bride has to give her name, age and occupation and her father's name and occupation. Work out the terminology, so you don't hesitate over whether you should be writing clerk or civil servant. In both register office and churches the bride should not be more than ten minutes late, because she could be delaying another wedding.

## REGISTER OFFICE MARRIAGE, SCOTLAND

You could marry at a register office anywhere in Scotland. For forms, write to General Register Office, New Register House, Edinburgh EH1 3YT, tel. 031–556 3952.

Gretna Green's popularity dates from the days when the age of consent was lower in Scotland than in England, and being just across the border it was the first place that runaway couples reached. Gretna is still such a popular venue for weddings that there is a three-month waiting list. You can wear what you like at the register office. Write to Gretna Green Register Office, 50A Annan Road, Gretna Green, Carlisle, tel. 0461 37648.

## RELIGIOUS CEREMONIES

### CHURCH OF ENGLAND

Allow enough time for the banns to be read on three successive Sundays beforehand – at least three weeks, depending on which day of the week you marry – and for residence requirements.

You will meet the vicar in advance to discuss and decide the wording of your marriage vows. The well-known traditional wording of the formula goes, 'Will you take ... ?' with the responses, 'I will ... with all my wordly goods I thee endow ... with my body I thee worship ... for better for worse ... till death do us part ...' You can either repeat each phrase of the reply after the vicar, or he can read the paragraph as a question to which you reply in the affirmative. It is nowadays less popular for the bride to promise to obey so you can omit this phrase. There is also a modern service with different wording.

The traditional service is in the prayer book you can obtain from your church. For full information consult your vicar. Details are given in the companion book to this, *Wedding Etiquette*. Or contact Church of England Enquiry Centre, Great Smith Street, Westminster, London SW1P 3NZ, tel. 01–222 9011. The Archbishop of Canterbury, resides at Lambeth Palace, London SE1 7JU, tel. 01–928 8282.

## CHOOSING CHURCH MUSIC

The traditional music 'Here Comes the Bride' is Wagner's *Wedding March* or *Bridal Chorus* from the opera *Lohengrin*. The wedding march for the recession down the aisle is from Mendelssohn's *Midsummer Night's Dream*. The pieces were chosen by Queen Victoria's eldest daughter for her wedding and have been popular ever since. An alternative to 'Here Comes the Bride' is Handel's *Arrival of the Queen of Sheba*.

Suitable hymns include *Amazing Grace*. For the recession Clarke's *Trumpet Voluntary* can be played. You may need music while waiting for the bride's arrival, and during the signing of the register (e.g. *Ave Maria*). The organist can offer suggestions and a hymn book to look at. (The organist is probably rather tired of playing 'Here Comes the Bride' and may try to encourage you to make a more original choice of music.)

Sheet music is obtainable from music shops. The *Alternative Service Book* contains the titles and words for many popular hymns, and psalms such as the 23rd psalm 'The Lord is my shepherd ...' .

## GUARD OF HONOUR

On emerging from the church the couple can be greeted by an avenue of well-wishers wearing uniform, often raising arms and symbols to form an arch. Army, Navy or Air Force officers raise ceremonial swords. Police raise truncheons. A cricket team raises bats. Adult schoolfriends wear the old school tie. Students raise scarves aloft. Schoolchildren, Boy Scouts and Cubs hold up hats or caps.

## WIDOWS AND WIDOWERS

A son can give the bride away, or her future father-in-law, uncle, friend, or a woman. Daughters and grand-children can be bridesmaids. Widows and widowers may marry in church.

## SECOND MARRIAGE FOR A DIVORCEE

Discuss with the minister what is acceptable to him. A service of blessing can be held with an address by the vicar, hymns and prayers and candles in church, and the men wearing morning suits. The bride's dress is usually not ankle-length white (the vicar may say this is inappropriate because the ceremony is not a wedding) but can be something equally pretty such as pale blue satin. One couple had a beautifully decorated church with flares along the country church path in midwinter. This can be followed by a reception as romantic and elaborate as you like.

## CHURCH OF SCOTLAND

Scottish couples marrying in church may dress in formal Scottish attire. For the ceremony a day jacket of tweed is worn, changed after 6 pm into a black jacket. A daytime hunting McKenzie kilt would be changed to dress McKenzie. Lace-up shoes are modern. The authentic Scottish shoe is a heavy brogue. The brown leather day sporran is rough and hairy. A leather Prince Charles sporran with silver gilt decoration is suitable for evening.

For details contact Church of Scotland, Enquiry Dept, 121 George Street, Edinburgh EH2 4YN, tel. 031–225 5722.

## IRISH WEDDINGS

For Irish weddings you can wear the tan colour Irish kilt and the Tara brooch worn by men and women. An

Irish piper (there are Irish Guards in London) can pipe the bride from church to car, and as she emerges from the car to the reception. He will wear the kilt, a green shawl, and tam-o'-shanter (bobble hat).

## ROMAN CATHOLIC

The wedding service and nuptial mass may take over an hour. A copy of the wedding service and nuptial mass can be obtained from Mowbrays bookshop in London. For more details contact The Catholic Marriage Advisory Council, London Centre, 23 Kensington Square, London W8, tel. 01 937 3781. You may wish to place a wedding announcement in a Catholic newspaper.

## ANGLO-CATHOLIC

Holy Communion may be part of the wedding service if you are deeply committed.

## NON-CONFORMIST AND FREE CHURCHES

Non-conformists are Protestant dissenters. Non-conformist weddings are an option for couples of mixed religion or from two churches – middle ground when neither wants to impose their ritual on the other.

The Free Churches (i.e. those outside the established Roman Catholic Church and Church of England) include Presbyterian (the main Church of Scotland), the Methodist, Baptists, Quaker, the United Reformed Church, and Pentecostal.

## METHODIST CHURCH

The Methodist Church is the largest of the Free Churches. You do not have to be a Methodist or even a Christian to marry in a Methodist church. Christians marrying Christians from other Churches or marrying Sikhs, Jews or Muslims might ask Methodist ministers to marry them. Discuss it with the minister. Methodists will marry divorced people but each minister may use their own discretion. Some ministers will marry a divorced person in church if they are the one deemed 'innocent'.

In a Methodist church you are married by a minister who explains what you have to do. You have your back to the congregation, and the minister is close enough to whisper instructions so it is almost impossible to make a mistake. Kneeling is optional, and your decision may depend on your wedding clothes. You could kneel for blessing at the end of the ceremony.

A registrar is not needed. The minister acts as registrar. The minister will explain everything to you. He will want to see you two or three times and talk about marriage. At many churches classes are held where you meet other couples.

## QUAKER WEDDINGS

For a wedding which is less basic than a register office if you cannot qualify for the Catholic or Anglican Church consider the Quakers. The Quakers return to the simplicity and peacefulness of the early days of Christianity, with no appointed ministers, no symbols, no creeds, hymns, nor set prayers.

An application to the Registering Officer of the monthly meeting to be held in the bride's home area must be made at least six weeks in advance. If the couple to be married are not Friends they must have attended meetings or be in sympathy with Quaker philosophy and two Friends must write in support of their application. A certificate has to be obtained from the Superintendent Registrar. The forthcoming marriage is then announced at a meeting, in the same way as banns are read in the Church of England. Assuming that there are no objections, those at the meeting set a date for a meeting when the marriage will be solemnized.

A marriage certificate is signed by the couple and two witnesses and read aloud. It is kept by the couple. Then the register is signed by all four and the Registering Officer.

For more details contact the Religious Society of Friends, Friends House, Euston Road, London NW1 2BJ, tel. 01 387 3601, or their Registering Officer. A leaflet called *Your First Time at a Quaker Meeting* is available from Quaker Home Service in London. Send guests a leaflet explaining Quaker meetings with invitations, so that they know what to expect. Different regulations apply in Scotland.

## EUROPEAN CHRISTIAN WEDDINGS

A civil ceremony normally takes place first.

## JEWISH WEDDINGS

Jewish weddings are often large with many guests — and increasingly non-Jewish guests.

### WHEN AND WHERE

Jewish weddings are held on Sunday or weekdays, not on the Sabbath (Saturday) which would interfere with religious services, nor on major holy days such as Yom Kippur, an autumn day of fasting. Extremely orthodox Jews do not travel on the Sabbath which starts and ends at dusk, affecting the timing of the wedding on Friday night in winter, and Saturday night in summer.

Unlike Christian church weddings which should be in daylight, Jewish tradition favours weddings late in the day with a view of the sky. In the UK, weddings are often held late in the day followed by a seated evening dinner-dance at a large hotel.

One couple whose families lived near each other, but who attended different synagogues, chose a third synagogue and invited the rabbis from the other two synagogues to attend.

In Israel, evening weddings take place in the open air under the stars. They may be in hotels with a canopy for the ceremony on the terrace. If marrying or honeymooning in Israel note that El Al does not fly on the Sabbath.

## BEFOREHAND

Before a wedding, an orthodox rabbi might require the bride to take a *mikva*, a ritual bath involving total immersion, rather like baptism, for symbolic purification. A bride who is reluctant might be asked to go away and think about it. Another rabbi might be less insistent on this.

Orthodox brides and grooms fast until the ceremony, to start marriage afresh. The groom must not be intoxicated or the marriage ceremony is invalid.

## JEWISH SECOND MARRIAGE

The secular divorce allows a Jewish woman to remarry in a register office. A Jewish divorcee wishing to remarry and have her second marriage recognised under Jewish law needs a *Get* or divorce document, issued by rabbinical authorities if the husband agrees to divorce. The *Get* enables her second marriage to be recognized and the children to be legitimate under Jewish law.

The Reform synagogues allow men and women to sit together, and use English language for about half the service. The Liberals are even more Anglicized and modernized, eating pork and appointing women rabbis.

Debate continues about the status of the children of non-orthodox Jews, and children of a Cohen (the name means priest), who is not supposed to marry a divorcee. More information can be obtained from The Chief Rabbi who has written a booklet about the marriage service, from your local Rabbi, synagogue office secretary, or the *Jewish Wedding Book*.

## MUSLIM WEDDINGS

The day before the wedding the Muslim girl has her hair and body prepared to look as attractive as possible, and her hands are decorated with red patterns. Orthodox weddings take place on an auspicious day such as the birthday of the prophet, at night, e.g. 8.30 pm. You can hold a wedding on a Friday, but not on a sad day commemorating martyrdom or the first month of the Islamic year. Two witnesses are appointed from each family – four in all. The boy's side provides the girl's white or red saree, lots of jewellery, perfumes, and fresh flower garlands. Her family provides his clothes.

Guests should remember that they will be removing their shoes and sitting on the floor in the mosque, so dress accordingly. The Islamic wedding is not necessarily held in the mosque but perhaps in the girl's house. Men and women, including the boy and girl are in separate rooms. The religious leader who supervizes goes to the girl who is asked if she accepts the boy and she nods three times.

Under Islamic law a man must wait until his first wife has had three menstrual periods before he embarks on a divorce. This is in order to ensure that the first wife is not bearing another child.

More details on Sunni weddings can be obtained from the Regents Park Mosque in London. A Shia centre is based in Stanmore, Middlesex.

## HINDU HOSTS AND GUESTS

Marriage takes place at a register office, then a Hindu temple where the priest officiates. He chooses an auspicious day depending on the couple's horoscopes.

## SIKH CEREMONIES

Sikhs have arranged marriages. After the register office marriage the Sikh wedding is held at a weekend or on a bank holiday at a Sikh temple.

## BAHAIS

When marrying a Bahai, you can have a Bahai wedding and then a church wedding, as the Bahais have no objection. Anyone who believes in one God can marry in the Bahai faith. They accept the founders of all the monotheistic religions, Moses, Jesus, Mohammed, and their own leader.

The Bahai national centre is in London but Bahais are scattered throughout Britain. There is a House of Worship on each continent – the main one being in Haifa, Israel, but few people are near one and most weddings take place in a home or hotel. The wedding is presided over by a member or elected officer of the local spiritual assembly.

You need a register office certificate. In Scotland the Bahai wedding is recognized and no extra civil ceremony is necessary, so Bahai officers officiate. But in England a register office marriage takes place first. The Bahai organization in London can supply a book called *Marriage: A fortress for well-being*.

## BUDDHIST

Sri Lankan Buddhist weddings take place in the home, not related to religious ceremonies, though a few prayers might be said. An auspicious day and auspicious time of day is chosen.

## ORIENTAL

The Japanese may hold the traditional Japanese wedding with the bride and groom both wearing kimonos, the bride having her face made up chalk white, or a Western-style wedding. The Japanese bride is expected to wear up to five outfits for the wedding day, where a display of the family's wealth is customary. The Japanese bride is likely to marry in a hotel under low lighting so wedding dresses decorated with elaborate beads would be appropriate. (See also **Wedding Gifts**, p. 113.)

## MIXED-FAITH MARRIAGES

(See notes above on Register Office, Free Church, and Bahai ceremonies. Non-conformist weddings are an advantage to those of mixed religion.)

People of liberal views often marry with the blessing of both families, but the orthodox may require conversion before you can be married on their premises. Technically some religious premises are licensed to marry only people of their own religion, therefore one or both of you must say that you follow that religion. This sometimes requires merely a nod as the secretary fills out an application form for you, your signature on the form and a non-committal declaration of belief in one God during the ceremony.

Rules vary with the allegiance of the congregation,

and the liberality of the minister. Ask before committing yourself to a particular church or minister. If you are shy about offending the Head of the Church or the Chief Rabbi by raising difficulties, speak to their secretary.

## ROMAN CATHOLIC RULES

Traditionally the spouse of a Catholic was required to convert but this is no longer the case. Roman Catholics in the UK do not require children to be brought up in the Roman Catholic faith, but they require the Roman Catholic partner to be strongly committed to seeing that the children have an opportunity to be Catholic. You may be required to state your intention to do so before you can get married. Discuss whether you are happy for one or both parties to agree to this. Some mixed-marriage couples bring children up learning about both faiths. Check by sending for the available literature. You may be able to have a ceremony with Christian ministers of Catholic and Protestant beliefs present.

## JEWISH RULES

The non-Jewish bride-to-be is expected to convert to Judaism because the children are only considered Jewish if they have a Jewish mother. She spends time learning how to run a Jewish home so that she can buy and cook kosher meat, light candles and say the Hebrew prayers over them for the Friday night family meal welcoming the start of the Sabbath. It is easier to convert into the liberal synagogue than into the orthodox one, and it is easier to convert in the US. It is easier to marry in a liberal synagogue than in an orthodox one. To be married in an orthodox synagogue in the UK you have to prove that your parents were married in an orthodox Jewish manner, e.g. by presenting a document showing that they married in an orthodox synagogue, not a liberal one. Converts may prefer to marry in an orthodox synagogue to protect their children from doubts raised later because one parent was a convert. Rules may change, so check with the Chief Rabbi's office in London. (See also **The Reception**.)

## ISLAMIC RULES

Under Islamic rules Muslim women may not marry a man from another faith but this is not the case for Muslim men. Muslim males can marry women from other monotheistic religions, Christian and Jewish. Sunni and Shiite Muslims have different rulings on morganatic marriages which prevent the children of morganatic wives inheriting (morganatic means morning, i.e. without full rights). Shiites accept morganatic marriages, which would affect a man who has up to four wives (in another country). A Muslim cannot marry a mother and daughter simultaneously. An agreement to refrain from polygamy can be written into a marriage contract. Check with the Regents Park Mosque in London or your local authorities.

Register office address ........................................................

.................................................................... Tel. ......................

Forms collected ..............................................................................

Documents ordered ........................................................................

Forms returned ................................................................................

Date of wedding ................................. Arrival time ................

Starting time ............................................ End time ......................

Minister's name and title ................................................................

........................................................................................................

His/Her home address ................................................................

................................................................ Fee ..........................

Other minister's name and title ................................................

Address ........................................................................................

........................................................................................................

Church/other premises address ................................................

................................................................ Tel. ..........................

Fee to join congregation ............................................................

Annual fee ..................................................................................

Payment/donation for wedding ................................................

Date ..............................................................................................

**Timing**

Groom's car arrives at ................................................................

Bride's car arrives at ..................................................................

For ceremony starts at ................................................................

Ceremony ends at ......................................................................

Bride's car departs at ................................................................

Last guest leaves at ....................................................................

Organist's name ..........................................................................

Address ........................................................................................

Tel. ................................................................ Fee ..........................

# TRANSPORT

For out-of-town guests, photocopy a map marking the route into town from your guests' direction of arrival.

If you anticipate 100 or so cars arriving simultaneously at the hotel reception ask if the hotel can provide two doormen to open both car doors and speed up the exit of guests from cars.

## TRANSPORT TO CHURCH/REGISTER OFFICE

Alternatives to the traditional Rolls are a Daimler or a Bentley. It is not unknown for the hire company to say that the car has broken down and send another colour and model. Check in advance how many vehicles they have, what substitution would be made in the event of a breakdown, and whether they will give a discount if they cannot supply the exact car booked. Confirm in writing. Most companies put white ribbon on the car; some additionally place silk flowers on the parcel shelf.

If you are using the groom or best man's car, arrange the following: Clean the car outside and inside. Fill the car up with petrol. Have the boot sufficiently clean for transporting wedding clothes. Keep a second set of car keys in a designated place in case the first set gets locked in the car boot or falls down a drain. Buy white ribbon and decide where to tie it. (A Rolls-Royce has the Silver Lady on the front of the bonnet; streamlined cars have fewer places for tying ribbons.) Put items such as a shaving foam canister for decorating the car in a box in the car boot.

If the best man is driving the groom's car he should take the car along the route and find out where he can park if there is a double yellow line outside the church. Calculate the time required for the journey in traffic. Learn how to operate reverse gear, unlock the car boot, remove the petrol cap, set and stop the car's burglar alarm. Obtain any needed car park ticket, parking disc or permit. Borrow the groom's garage key, or block of flats' security barrier card for returning the groom's car. Make a map for the guests.

## TRANSPORT TO RECEPTION

White is the popular wedding car colour but the bride's white dress and the car's white ribbons look more dramatic against royal blue or a dark colour. Using your own car means you have a chance to practise taking photos of the couple and the car. If the best man and groom do not have smart cars, review which friends own fancy cars, for example the bride's father's neighbour, or the groom's boss. For even more panache hire a horse and carriage, or make a novelty of an original vehicle you have available. Decoration required includes a white ribbon on the second wedding car.

### OTHER OPTIONS: TAXI/BUS

Black vintage taxis or white taxis can be hired.

To avoid parking problems in London a couple hired a red London bus from London Transport, complete with driver. They were not allowed to add white ribbons, but the photographs were amusing and distinctive anyway. The bus took the guests to the register office and on to a restaurant. Afterwards it collected everybody and took them back to the couple's home where their cars were parked.

## DECORATING THE DEPARTURE VEHICLE

Best man and ushers should stock up with car decoration equipment. Make a 'Just Married' sign. Get old shoes or boots and ribbon. Buy spray-on foam.

Bridesmaids can remove flowers from bouquets, attaching them to the car with wires. Lipstick can be used to write slogans on windows (not chemicals on car paint!) such as: 'It's Legal', 'Off To Get A Little Sun And Air', 'Wave If She's Pretty'.

Foam signs can be removed with window cleaner, or petrol if all else fails. Have a cloth handy in the boot for wiping off 'Just Married' signs which might obscure vision.

The newlyweds might depart with cans tied onto a hired motorcaravan used for their honeymoon, visiting distant family, taking champagne and cake to those who could not attend the wedding.

## GOING AWAY CAR

Check that the bride's going away outfit is suitably stylish or amusing, appropriate for the going away vehicle, especially if it is unusual. Astride a tandem or motorbike she should avoid wearing a tight skirt. A hat needs an anchor clip or ribbons. Without a hand free for her clutch bag or handbag she needs a shoulder bag. If the couple are riding off on a motorbike, they should decide who is transporting the luggage.

When the bride and groom are not changing into going away outfits the car must be decorated quickly.

Paint a 'Just Married' card in advance. Sellotape on a balloon or two – perhaps borrowed from the reception decorations.

## COPING WITH PRACTICAL JOKES

If the groom's friends include many jokers planning such tricks as spreading flour over the car handles they should drop heavy hints before the wedding, 'you will be surprised ...'. Then the best man can help the groom to avoid damage to his new car by borrowing an obliging friend's beat-up croc for the going-away car.

Jokers may spray the car with shaving foam, and padlock chains and bells onto the bumper – you will need to find a garage with a hacksaw to remove these. If you use the best man's car, he can take the padlock key and remove the chains later. Drive to a nearby house in the decorated car. Let the best man explain to the clothes hire company why the clothes are daubed with flour (serves him right) while the laughing bride and calm, unflappable groom transfer to a smart car or hire car. (Best man, or groom, must ensure all luggage and vital documents go into the second car!)

## FOREIGN WEDDING CUSTOMS TO COPY

You might copy some ideas from Europe. On the continent a Mercedes, a VW, or a vintage car is popular as a wedding car. The bride's bouquet might be placed on the bonnet.

### EUROPEAN DECORATION

In Europe cars are decorated differently. A small car would be decorated with bows made from strips of white ribbon, net, lace, or muslin. Bows are tied to the two upright sections on the front bumper. The main ribbon crosses from the windscreen wipers to the front headlights, making an X or upside V. A bow is tied in the middle between the windscreen wipers, and more bows where the ends are attached to the headlights. Bows can be tied to the car aerial.

In France and Italy, flowers are put around the inside of the window frames so they are visible from outside, as well as on the back parcel shelf.

In the country in Switzerland they make arches over the village street hung with items relating to the bride and groom, e.g. baby clothes for a nurse, whisks and wooden spoons for a chef. The bride and groom might roll-up to the reception dining room door on a restaurant kitchen trolley, or the hotel's luggage trolley. Usually they arrive local style, in winter on skis, by helicopter borrowed from helicopter-ski schools, in sledges covered with fur rugs, or horse-drawn sleighs with sleighbells.

### TRANSPORT AND DECORATION IN ISRAEL

Fresh flowers in geometric patterns decorate wedding cars in Israel. White balloons can be tied to the bumpers and roof. Bridal couples drive around Jerusalem in a horse and carriage being photographed at picturesque holy sites before reaching the reception. You could do the same in English cities or seasides.

### MUSLIM TRANSPORT DECORATION

The groom's car is decorated to take him to the mosque, and the same car takes the bride and groom from the ceremony to the reception.

### HINDU TRANSPORT DECORATION

The priest places a painted coconut, symbol of life, before the car, which is colourfully decorated with red ribbons, balloons, or commercial giftwrap bows.

## TRANSPORT CHECKLIST

Check that you know all of the following details about your transport: Vehicle/chauffeur/driver/owner or hire company name/address/tel.

For bride/groom/family/guests/collect from address/

time/deliver to address/decoration/charge/period of hire/
extra charges/insurance/petrol/tips.

| HIRE COMPANY |
|---|

Name ................................................................................................

Address ...........................................................................................

.................................................................... Tel. .............................

Acceptable/Not acceptable (reason) .........................................

.................................................... Family informed   No/Yes.

Booking made by phone   No/Yes.   Booking in writing

No/Yes. By (name) .........................................................................

Date   ....................   To (name) ................................................

Written confirmation received   No/Yes (date) ................

From (name) ...................................................................................

Insurance .........................................................................................

# PLANNING THE WEDDING RECEPTION

## WHERE TO HOLD THE RECEPTION

Home or away? Marquees in city gardens or country fields offer you the option of seated meals or buffets. Halls and hotels are ideal for sit-down meals. So are barns, stately homes, and baronial halls. The first thing to do is make an early booking of the hall.

## PROFESSIONAL CATERING

The size of the wedding reception affects the time spent selecting a caterer. Agree the menu including alternatives for dieters and vegetarians. Confirm everything in writing, including whether waiters serve buffet only or all drinks and food at tables, service charge, expected additional tipping, and VAT.

### SCOTLAND

You can order heart-shape cakes at Gretna Chase Hotel on the English side of the border for Valentine's Day when five or six marriages take place with hotel receptions, and couples book four-poster beds or bridal suites.

The minister is master of ceremonies/compère. The

minister and his wife sit at either end of the top table normally but at a Scottish wedding the minister sits centrally next to the bride. A ceilidh band with a fiddle and accordion play Scottish dances, no disco music or waltzes. Food will be cock-o-leekie soup or Cullen skink (Scottish fish soup), haggis or Aberdeen Angus beef, dessert of Atholl brose or cranachan — whisky, cream, honey and oats.

## IRISH RECEPTION

Irish whiskey can be served at the start of the reception and at the end, neat or mixed with Guinness to make 'Black Velvet'.

## JEWISH RECEPTION

Kosher food requires supervision of the products by rabbinical authorities, and preparation in a kosher kitchen, where neither crockery nor food are contaminated by non-kosher food (pork and shellfish). Large hotels have arrangements with kosher caterers who will either steam-clean the kitchen or cover surfaces with cloth for the day.

A typical meal might include smoked salmon or melon, kosher chicken or meat, dessert without lard (avoid pork products). Several London restaurants provide kosher catering.

Fish (not shellfish) and fruit, with pretty paper plates and cups could be used to supplement a meal catered at home if you have guests requiring ethnic food.

## MUSLIM RECEPTION

No pork is served, only halal meat, and no alcohol. Western-style wedding cake with the cake-cutting ceremony is popular. There are no toasts but a speech may be made by the groom's family, welcoming guests who have made the effort to travel from afar; the groom may speak, complimenting the bride. Guests should dress prepared to sit on a carpeted floor.

## HINDU RECEPTION

There may be hundreds of guests so a video enables hosts to enjoy seeing who was there. Hindu brides live with the mother-in-law. Non-Hindu brides whose vegetarian mother-in-law comes to stay from overseas need cooking pans which have not been used for meat. Salt is used to scrub fat off a frying pan used for bacon, or new pans are bought.

## DRINKS

A trade rule is half a bottle of wine per person. However, the amount of alcohol consumed varies according to the reception's length and quantity of food. Offer aperitifs such as sherry, and later drinks such as white wine with the food. Include different brands of beer, mixers, rosé and sweet wines, low-alcohol drinks like Kaliber from Guinness, a 1% alcohol from Bass, and Diet Coke. Champagne or sparkling wine is needed for the toasts. Children can be given Perrier, fruit juice or soda water. Provide ice buckets.

## CATERERS

Name ...............................................................................................................

Address .........................................................................................................

........................................................................... Tel. ..............................

Meal prices .................................................................................................

Drink prices .................................................................................................

Other extras .................................................................................................

Notes ..............................................................................................

Acceptable/Not acceptable (reason ........................................

.......................................................... ). Family informed   No/Yes.

Booking made by phone   No/Yes.   Booking in writing

No/Yes.   By (name) ...................................................................

Date ...................... To (name) ...........................................................

Written confirmation received   No/Yes (date) ...................

From (name) ...................................................................................

Insurance ..........................................................................................

## BUDGET CELEBRATION

If you have no budget at all, follow your register office wedding with a restaurant meal. Send your small number of guests a handwritten note in advance saying, 'Mary and I will be celebrating by having a meal at Antonio's Italian Restaurant in the High Street at 7 pm. The cost will be about £10 per head and if you would care to join us we shall be delighted to see you.'

If you feel it is an imposition to ask friends to pay for their own meal and want a quiet wedding, you can have a register office wedding somewhere remote and far from where you live. Then celebrate on your own in a hotel with a four-poster bed and order yourselves a super restaurant meal with a bottle of champagne.

## SELF-CATERING

Home-made cake can be iced professionally, or a bought cake can be decorated at home. Organize sufficient space for freezer storage – perhaps using neighbours' help. You can hire equipment, coat racks, seats, drinking glasses, etc. Plan the timing of making food, calculate time for laying tables, and whether serving staff are required.

## RECEPTIONS HELD AT HOME

If you are planning a marquee you need a large enough garden for the marquee suitable for the number of guests you are inviting. Have a wet weather plan and a fine weather plan for a home wedding reception. You may want a awning from the house to the marquee.

Ensure you have enough chairs and crockery, cutlery and drinking glasses. Glasses can be borrowed from off-licences. Collect glasses in advance so you don't find suppliers have run out on the day because other customers borrowed the lot. You need enough freezer or larder space for the cake and all the food. You may have to enlist the aid of neighbours, friends or relatives. Alternatively book a catering company who will turn up with the food on the day. If you are providing the tablecloths, fresh flowers or silk flower arrangements these should be in place well in advance of the caterers' arrival.

House guests can help with catering and preparing the home for a home wedding reception. Work out a rota for the use of the bathroom so that on the day the bride or groom has precedence. Everybody should keep their clothes, hairdriers, and toothbrushes in their bedrooms.

Make provision for the guests' clothes, a clear bed, an empty cupboard with spare hangers, or a borrowed or hired clothes rail (advertised in national newspapers).

Signs indicating locations within the house are useful, for example, coats upstairs (arrow pointing to staircase), toilet/gentlemen's toilet (arrow to downstairs cloakroom), ladies' coats and powder room (arrow to bedroom, second toilet/ladies' toilet (arrow to upstairs bathroom), drinks this way (arrow to kitchen), food this way (arrow to living room), photographer at end of garden by roses (arrow to French windows), marquee this way (arrow to side gate).

On a kitchen pinboard place a typed list of useful phone numbers such as the railway station, nearby hotel, car hire and so on. Or stick business cards from local taxi firms on a pinboard by the phone.

## SELECTING WEDDING CAKE

Traditional cakes have three tiers, five tiers with column supports, or simply each layer resting on the one below. Shapes include circular, square or heart-shaped. A miniature bride and groom can be placed on top, or a vase of fresh flowers. Sample the cake to check quality. Vegetarian wedding cakes without animal fats can be made to order at Harrods.

## EUROPEAN-STYLE RECEPTIONS

Wedding cakes are tiered white iced cakes but usually sponge cakes, not the heavy rich fruit cake which is used in Britain.

In France the centrepiece is a *pièce montée* (a mountainous piece), a pyramid of choux buns. Other reception food might include a tier of iced white trays on white columns, bearing different gateaux and pastries on each level.

In Italy guests are given small sweets, usually white and pink sugar-covered almonds in little muslin bags tied with ribbons or in porcelain boxes.

The Swiss reception might be decorated with candles, Christmas fairy lights, sparklers, and bubble blowing. The lights are turned out for the bride to enter to 'Here Comes the Bride', and ultra-violet light illuminates her white dress.

Cake supplier

Name .............................................................................................................

Address ........................................................................................................

............................................................................ Tel. ...........................

Prices ...........................................................................................................

Dates and times ........................................................................................

Notes ...........................................................................................................

............................................................................................................................

Acceptable/Not acceptable (reason ......................................................

.................................................. ). Family informed No/Yes.

Booking made by phone No/Yes. Booking in writing

No/Yes. By (name) ....................................................................................

Date ...................... To (name) .............................................................

Written confirmation received No/Yes (date) ................

From (name) ...............................................................................................

Insurance ....................................................................................................

## TABLE DECORATION

You can have candles, printed menus, placecards, serviettes, crackers, matchbooks or balloons printed with names and date, and fancy paper plates. Partial buffet or full service may be provided. Check what will happen to leftover food and the tables' flower displays.

Can guests take the flower displays, or will flowers be saved for the bride, bride's mother, and mother-in-law?

## SEATING PLANS

Order at the top table is as follows. Bride and groom are seated in the centre with the groom on the bride's right. It is easier to identify who's who if his parents are next to him and hers are next to her. This is ideal for ethnic minority families where husband and wife are inseparable, or mixed-race marriages where his side can't talk to hers because of language or other cultural differences.

Alternatively follow traditional etiquette dividing the parents. Put the groom's mother-in-law on his right, and the bride's father on the bride's mother's right. This is thought to make conversation more interesting, since you can talk to your own family at home.

The caterer or stationer can draw up a seating plan with a printed edge and names written on by someone with good handwriting. If you have many guests display two copies of the plan.

Children over seven can be seated, under-sevens provided with a crèche. Hiring a childminder/communal babysitter for a couple of hours and getting pizzas delivered could be cheaper than ordering ten seated dinners which probably won't be eaten.

| SEATING |
| --- |

★ *TOP TABLE*

1 ..................................................................................................

2 ..................................................................................................

3 ..................................................................................................

4 ..................................................................................................

Bride ..................................................................................................

**Groom** ...................................................................................................
   **1** ...................................................................................................
   **2** ...................................................................................................
   **3** ...................................................................................................
   **4** ...................................................................................................

### ★ *HER FAMILY TABLE*
   **1** ...................................................................................................
   **2** ...................................................................................................
   **3** ...................................................................................................
   **4** ...................................................................................................
   **5** ...................................................................................................
   **6** ...................................................................................................
   **7** ...................................................................................................
   **8** ...................................................................................................
   **9** ...................................................................................................
 **10** ...................................................................................................

### ★ *HIS FAMILY TABLE*
   **1** ...................................................................................................
   **2** ...................................................................................................
   **3** ...................................................................................................
   **4** ...................................................................................................
   **5** ...................................................................................................
   **6** ...................................................................................................
   **7** ...................................................................................................
   **8** ...................................................................................................
   **9** ...................................................................................................
 **10** ...................................................................................................

### ★ *HER FRIENDS' TABLE*
   **1** ...................................................................................................
   **2** ...................................................................................................
   **3** ...................................................................................................
   **4** ...................................................................................................
   **5** ...................................................................................................

6 .................................................................................
7 .................................................................................
8 .................................................................................
9 .................................................................................
10 ................................................................................

★ *HIS FRIENDS' TABLE*

1 .................................................................................
2 .................................................................................
3 .................................................................................
4 .................................................................................
5 .................................................................................
6 .................................................................................
7 .................................................................................
8 .................................................................................
9 .................................................................................
10 ................................................................................

## TOASTMASTERS

Hotels and caterers can put you in touch with toastmasters, some of whom are part-timers. The Guild of Professional Toastmasters has over a dozen members who are trained or experienced full-time toastmasters with references. Their headquarters is in London, listed under Toastmasters in commercial telephone directories, but they may travel.

Toastmaster's name .................................................................

Address .......................................................................................

.................................................................... Tel. ...........................

Fee ................ Special instructions given ...........................

.................................................................................................

.................................................................................................

## CAKE CUTTING

After the meal people may be too full to eat cake but if you leave cake cutting until later everyone may have disappeared from the tables. Cutting the cake before the speeches gives the caterer time to cut the cake neatly while speeches are being made and serve it to fill the lull after speeches. If the meal is at lunchtime the wedding cake can be served with coffee at tea-time.

An engagement party or stag party held at home can be a dry run for the wedding reception. Work out where you have room for the receiving line. Be inventive. If the hall is tiny you could have the receiving line on the lawn alongside the front garden path. You can have it on the stairs if the house has a wide staircase. Alternatively have a maid in starched apron at the front door to show the guests where to put their coats, and the family standing in a receiving line on the back garden path, perhaps in front of the marquee. In addition to a marquee, you might use ribbons and stands to mark off a pathway.

## SPEECHES

Writing a speech can be fun. There are many source books for speech-writing and quotations, including my book *Wedding Speeches & Toasts* published in this series. The father's opening speech can take the theme of not losing a daughter but gaining a son, ending with a toast to the bride and groom.

An amusing speech can be created by having the groom's father join in, doing a double act like the comedians The Two Ronnies. 'Good evening, ladies and gentlemen,' says the bride's father, and the groom's father stands up beside him saying, 'And good evening from me, too'. An English family did this with the two fathers reading alternate lines of verse about their respective son and daughter. The groom's father finished second, 'and goodnight from me, too.'

The groom's response thanks his hosts. The groom returns the compliment by praising and thanking the bride's family and others who organized the wedding (nowadays praising his parents as well as the bride's) ending with a toast to the bridesmaids or if there are none he toasts his hosts (the bride's parents).

Enlist help from the families of the bride, groom, or attendants. One best man had his speech written in verse by the groom's mother. Include personal details and compliments about the people you are toasting. Insert brief anecdotes about how they met, their common interests, difficulties they overcame, and the setting or circumstances of the marriage proposal.

After thanking the groom on behalf of the bridesmaids, the best man's speech is expected to be amusing. He might read the day's weather forecast adapted, 'Wedding Day started fair, hotter towards evening, forecast for future very bright,' present a gift such as two chef's hats, a giant envelope labelled Virility Test, or Writ, or

Recorded Delivery (photograph groom signing for receiving it). It could contain a giant photograph of the bride and groom, enormous congratulations card or telegram.

The best man and chief bridesmaid can share a speech, reading alternating paragraphs about the groom's childhood, the bride's, his career and hers, his good qualities and hers, his ambitions, and hers. This is amusing and easier than making a long speech alone. You can also buy a professional speech for a modest cost. Advertisements are found in bridal magazines.

Delivering a speech requires practice. Do a test recording of your speech to check that you are not gabbling too fast, droning slowly, or umming and arring. Also avoid jangling coins in your pockets during your speech and anybody else's.

A professional video firm will record the speeches. Or an ordinary hand-held micro-cassette recorder can be used to make an amateur recording.

Speeches to be given by:

1 .......................................................................................................

2 .......................................................................................................

3 .......................................................................................................

Amateur/professional speechwriter giving help ................

.......................................................................................................

.......................................................................................................

My speech researched/handwritten/typed/kept in ............

.......................................................................................................

.......................................................................................................

## PHOTOGRAPHS

### AMATEUR PHOTOGRAPHY

Ensure amateurs have equipment including tripod, flashgun, spare batteries, and plenty of film. You should probably reimburse the photographer for the cost of the film or provide it yourself. Have at least two cameras in case one jams.

Camera ................................ New batteries ....................

Flash ........................................................ Tripod ....................

Film ................................................................ Cost ..................

The best man can send an usher to the high street one-hour photograph developers and get photographs back in time to show the couple and guests. Retake the poorer shots and order duplicates of the successful ones.

Developing and printing service company

Name ...............................................................................................

Address ...........................................................................................

............................................................ Tel. ...............................

Date and time for collecting prints ...........................................

Wedding album cost ................... Duplicate cost ..................

You can order dulpicate sets of colour prints by post. Envelopes are displayed at post offices and airports. Colour slides which include processing can be posted on the wedding day or by the best man the next day in time for the slides to be on the doormat when the bride and groom return from their honeymoon.

## SELECTING PROFESSIONAL PHOTOGRAPHERS

Look at friends' wedding albums. See two or three photographers and their sample books and get written estimates of cost before deciding. Some photographers operate on an hourly basis. Others make a minimum charge, plus a charge for the number of photographs ordered. They might offer a leather album filled with a certain number of prints. There could be no obligation, just a choice of packages, with the option of deciding which to accept after you have seen the photographs. Check whether you are getting a specific photographer or one of the company's team.

## PHOTOGRAPH SUBJECT CHECKLIST

☆ Photographs of bride alone and with parents at her home.

☆ Bride (and father) in wedding car outside their house.

☆ Bride arriving at church/register office.

☆ Procession.

☆ Altar.

☆ Signing register.

☆ Recession.

☆ On church steps with minister and all the guests.

☆ Bride and groom kissing or hugging in car.

☆ Bridal party in garden of reception venue.

☆ Bridal party at top table.

☆ Cake cutting.

☆ Speechmakers.

☆ Selected guests. (Tell photographer about VIPs such as granny.)

☆ Bride and groom at top of stairs with bride's dress and train draped down stairs.

☆ Bride and groom with both sets of parents.

☆ Bride and female attendants.

☆ Groom with best man and ushers.

☆ Wedding present display (useful for insurance).

☆ Bride and groom in going away outfits standing with new luggage by wedding car.

☆ Bride and groom waving from wedding car through open doors or windows.

Ask if the photographer will stay right to the end. If the hotel room is nearby he can photograph bride and groom in the four-poster bed or jacuzzi with the champagne, or in the bedroom or living room of the new home. Studio pictures can be taken of the bride in her wedding dress before or after the wedding.

Some photographers develop the films on the wedding day and cheaply reprint group photographs in bulk for all the guests. Pictures can be enlarged to poster-size for framing and hanging on the wall. Photographs can be printed to look like oil paintings, or transferred onto souvenir plates, tablemats, key-rings, and jigsaws (for the junior bridesmaid and pageboy). You can also have stills made from a video film.

## VIDEOTAPING

Choose the hire company after viewing their film and

comparing the cost of videotape with and without a soundtrack. Specify the order of main scenes. Decide how leftover film will be finished, by taking randomly selected dancing guests, or more photos of bride and groom. Find out the cost of a duplicate film for parents.

Photography/Video firm name ...........................................................

Address ...............................................................................................

........................................................................ Tel. ...........................

Special instructions ...........................................................................

.............................................................................................................

Acceptable/Not acceptable (reason) ...............................................

......................................................... Family informed   No/Yes.

Booking made by phone   No/Yes.   Booking in writing

No/Yes.   By (name) ........................................................................

Date ...................... To (name) ......................................................

Written confirmation received   No/Yes (date) .................

From (name) .......................................................................................

Alternative company ........................................................................

## ENTERTAINMENT

### LIVE MUSIC

You might ask a relative with a lovely voice to sing, or engage a band specializing in local music, or an unusual instrument to play a solo at the wedding reception. Some possibilities are: a pianist, harpist, string quartet or clarinettist, guitar or accordion player, choirboy, church choir, a school or university group, a Scottish piper, a Welsh male voice choir, Irish piper and fiddler,

Caribbean or Greek band, band with trumpet player. Specialist firms supply musical groups.

Musicians should be asked to play quietly so guests can talk during the greeting of guests at the receiving line. Guests take their places at table or wait by the buffet until the bride enters last, often announced by the playing of 'Here Comes the Bride'. During the meal, mood music can be played.

## WEDDING THEME SONGS

Wedding theme songs are *Congratulations* (Cliff Richard), *Love And Marriage* (Sammy Cahn), *Going To The Chapel*, *Get Me To The Church On Time* (My Fair Lady), *The Wedding Song* (Peter, Paul & Mary), *Kiss The Bride* (Elton John), *Hawaiian Wedding Song* (Elvis, Andy Williams and others) and *I'm A Believer* (The Monkees).

## PERSONAL SONGS

Caribbean Calypso singers and Welsh singers can make up songs including the bride's name or groom's characteristics. Many songs already exist, e.g. for the bride *Annie's Song* (John Denver), *Michelle* (The Beatles), *Diana* (Paul Anka), *Sara* (Fleetwood Mac), *Looking For Linda* (Hue and Cry). For the groom the singer, disc jockey or best man can make a jokey compendium: *He's My Blue Eyed Boy* (Piaf), *You're So Vain* (Carly Simon). If the bride and groom cannot already say 'they're playing our song', find them a happy song like *Beautiful Day*, or one fitting the wedding day weather such as *Sunshine Of My Life*, *Singing In The Rain*, or *White Christmas*.

## SENTIMENTAL MUSIC

Include songs everyone knows so they can join in

choruses. Romantic slow music is obtainable on record collections of love songs such as *Endless Love*. Include nostalgic snatches of songs from the wedding period of the bride's and groom's parents and grandparents, such as Victorian *Daisy Daisy, Give Me Your Answer Do.*

## BRITISH ISLES REGIONAL

Pick regional music from the wedding location. For example, English songs include *Maybe It's Because I'm A Londoner* or *You'll Never Walk Alone*. Scottish favourites include *A Gordon For Me*, *Gay Gordons*, *Mull of Kintyre*, and *Skye Boat Song*. For Welsh guests select a mixture of Welsh harp music or traditional songs such as *Men Of Harlech* and *The Ashgrove*. Irish songs include *When Irish Eyes Are Smiling*, Irish reels, and *Danny Boy* (unofficial national anthem for Northern Ireland and Eire).

## NATIONAL AND INTERNATIONAL

(Homeland and Honeymoon.)

Add national songs from the homeland of hosts and guests, or the honeymoon location. West Indian brides or those taking an exotic honeymoon might like the Caribbean song *Island In The Sun* (Harry Belafonte), or reggae. Australia's *Waltzing Mathilda* is popular. American music includes *If You're Going To San Francisco*, *New York New York*, *Chicago*, *America The Beautiful* and *Dixie*. Wordsheets accompany cassettes or records in music shops, or use library song directories.

Songs evoking European honeymoon locations include French, *I Love Paris In The Springtime*, or *After They've Seen Paree*. Italian music varies from Schubert's *Ave Maria* (Caruso), to *Que Sera Sera* (Whatever Will Be Will Be), *Dimmi Quando Quando*

*Quando* (Tell Me When). The Spanish favourite is *Que Viva Espana*.

## DANCING

A drum roll is sounded before the first dance, traditionally the *Anniversary Waltz*, with the bride and groom starting the dancing.

### SUGGESTED DANCES

Include party dances such as the Conga, the Twist, and the Charleston. For your exhibitionist guests play the Tango, and the Gezutski (a fast Russian dance, squatting, with your arms crossed and alternating each leg forward until exhausted!). Flamenco is jolly for a dance or two, especially if you provide castanets. Greek music, particularly *Zorba's Dance*, will encourage group dancing. So will the rousing Israeli *Hava Na Gila* danced to the Hora. Latin American Sambas and Rumbas are also lively. Communal dances such as the Hokey Cokey enable guests lacking dancing partners to join the fun. Children like *The Birdie Song*.

### DANCE MUSIC VOLUME

Older people often prefer music quiet enough to enable them to exchange gossip. Check early in the evening that older people sitting talking are not shouting themselves hoarse. If so, ask the hotel manager whether he can switch off some of the speakers.

## DISCO MUSIC

A separate disco can be held later in the day for the young people. At home you can provide music by hiring a live band, or a mobile discotheque. Discuss how loudly they will play, ensuring that the music will not deafen you and annoy neighbours. Ask for a list of suggestions and give them a list of your favourite songs. Supply them with discs they do not stock which you would like played.

## RECORDED MUSIC

If there is insufficient space for a band you can use your own record player. Go through your cassettes and records and put suitable ones in order, or perhaps record a selection of your favourites, mixing lively tracks with mood music.

If your stereo system or cassette player is not loud enough to be heard above a roomful of guests attach larger speakers. Music can be played on a piano or electric organ, perhaps with a guitarist. Check that the piano is tuned and select suitable music scores.

### LAST DANCE

If the band plans to finish dancing with a 'last waltz' the bride and groom should practice a waltz, especially if the bride has to whirl around in a long white dress and new shoes. End with relevant national songs or anthems such as the French *Marseillaise*. If you are playing the Israeli national anthem *Hatikva* or a Japanese song such as *Sayonara* (meaning good-bye), include a songsheet with the words in phonetics and translation. *God Save The Queen* is played last at elegant formal dinners, or for a merry conclusion, *Auld Lang Syne*.

Singer/band name  ..............................................................................

Address  ..............................................................................................

.................................................................  Tel.  ...............................

Cost ................................................................ Tips ..............................

Time of arrival ......................................................................................

Number of intervals ............................................................................

Length of intervals ..............................................................................

Time of departure ................................................................................

Substitute in case of illness/transport problems ................

.....................................................................................................................

Music shop name ................................................................................

Address ....................................................................................................

.......................................................................... Tel. ..............................

Music ordered ........................................................................................

Date .................................................................... Cost ..............................

# WEDDING GIFTS

## MAKING WEDDING LISTS

For a quickly arranged wedding with few guests the bride's mother can send out a simple list merely stating 'a tea set' and so on. If you have time, compose a full list with columns indicating Brand/Style/Colour alongside each item. If you give several people the same list you risk getting duplicate gifts. But if you wait for each person to tick and return the list before sending to another, some guests won't get the list and may forget to buy a gift! You could divide your list into three, or ask guests to buy from a particular department store, even though you have not made a list there.

Older couples may already have one or two sets of everything. In that case presents relating to their personal interest might be the solution. For example, a couple who have a dining table and a dinner service but play bridge might welcome a card table.

## CHOOSING A STORE'S GIFT LIST

Wedding lists can be placed at department stores or at specialized shops such as Chinacraft. Gifts can be delivered in advance, or all together to the new home after the wedding, or shipped directly abroad which can save VAT.

Harrods offers a 'Hold All Orders' option holding the money but usually sending goods all together up to 18 months after the wedding, allowing the bride to change her mind about any or all of them. Guests can order by phone. The purchase list is sent weekly so the bride can write thank you notes.

John Lewis, Oxford Street, and Peter Jones send a summary of gifts bought with donor's names at the end of the time period, which helps the bride to write thank you notes.

Items which must be installed before you move in can be bought with cheques from relatives who ask if you would prefer money.

Department Store name ......................................................................

Address ..........................................................................................

.......................................................... Tel. ..........................

Type of wedding list chosen ..........................................................

Deliver to ....................................................................................

.......................................................... Date ..........................

| WEDDING GIFT CHECKLIST |
| --- |

The Store/Department/Brand/Colour/Received/Donor/Thanked/Exchanged.

★ *INTERIOR*
  carpet ........................................................................ ☐
  curtains ...................................................................... ☐
  wallpaper .................................................................... ☐
  heaters ....................................................................... ☐
  light fittings ............................................................... ☐
  mirrors ....................................................................... ☐
  vacuum cleaner .......................................................... ☐
  wastebins ................................................................... ☐

secondary glazing ☐
curtain rails ☐

★ *EXTERIOR*
doorknocker ☐
bell ☐
house number ☐
dustbin ☐
shutters ☐
locks or burglar alarms ☐
outside lights ☐

★ *LIVING ROOMS*
settee and easy chairs ☐
dining table and chairs ☐
TV ☐
video ☐
pictures ☐
vases ☐
ornaments ☐
shelving or cabinets ☐
stacking coffee tables ☐
wine glasses ☐
sherry glasses ☐
coasters ☐
cakeslice and pastry forks ☐
carving set ☐
electric meat slicer ☐
coffee spoons ☐
grapefruit spoons ☐
serving spoons ☐
steak knives ☐
corn cob holders ☐
candlesticks ☐
cheeseboard ☐
toast rack ☐

cookery books .................................................. ☐
magazine rack .................................................. ☐
radio .................................................. ☐
cassette player .................................................. ☐
winerack .................................................. ☐
houseplants .................................................. ☐
cache-pots .................................................. ☐

★ *BEDROOMS*
bed .................................................. ☐
headboard .................................................. ☐
mattress .................................................. ☐
pillows .................................................. ☐
bedding .................................................. ☐
electric blanket .................................................. ☐
duvet .................................................. ☐
matching curtains .................................................. ☐
bedside tables .................................................. ☐
table lamps .................................................. ☐
alarm clock .................................................. ☐
teamaker .................................................. ☐
convertible guest bed .................................................. ☐

Cupboard fittings:
shelves .................................................. ☐
clothes rail and tie rack .................................................. ☐

★ *BATHROOM*
shower unit .................................................. ☐
blind .................................................. ☐
towels .................................................. ☐
bathroom cabinet .................................................. ☐

Accessory set including:
toothbrush holder .................................................. ☐
toilet paper holder .................................................. ☐
linen basket .................................................. ☐

bathroom scales ☐
hairdryer ☐
first aid kit ☐
bathmat ☐
shower rail ☐
shower curtain ☐
bidet ☐
taps ☐
extractor fan ☐

★ *KITCHEN*
fridge ☐
deep freeze ☐
oven ☐
hob ☐
extractor fan ☐
dishwasher ☐
microwave ☐
electric kettle ☐
tin opener ☐
bottle opener ☐
toaster ☐
foodmixer ☐
saucepans ☐
baking pans ☐
table and chairs ☐
tablecloth ☐
tablemats ☐
cruet ☐
cutlery ☐
crockery ☐
waterglasses ☐
jugs ☐
clock ☐
coffeemaker ☐
tea service ☐

tray ........................................................................... ☐
pinboard ................................................................... ☐
casserole dishes ..................................................... ☐
breadbin ................................................................... ☐
spice rack ................................................................ ☐
iron ........................................................................... ☐
ironing board .......................................................... ☐
freezer bag ............................................................. ☐

★ *GARDEN*
lawnmower .............................................................. ☐
wheelbarrow ........................................................... ☐
garden tools ........................................................... ☐
conifers ................................................................... ☐
fencing .................................................................... ☐
climbing plants ....................................................... ☐
fruit plants .............................................................. ☐
flower plants .......................................................... ☐
table ........................................................................ ☐
chairs ...................................................................... ☐
parasol .................................................................... ☐
sunloungers ............................................................ ☐
urns ......................................................................... ☐
statues .................................................................... ☐
barbecue ................................................................. ☐
hammock ................................................................. ☐
hedgetrimmer ......................................................... ☐
garden shed ............................................................ ☐
greenhouse ............................................................. ☐
watering can ........................................................... ☐
hose ......................................................................... ☐
sprinkler .................................................................. ☐

★ *BALCONY/PATIO*
folding director's chairs ......................................... ☐
small table .............................................................. ☐

plants ☐
clothes drying stand ☐
windowbox ☐
pair of reclining chairs ☐
hanging chair ☐

## ★ *GARAGE/UTILITY ROOM*
washing machine ☐
tumble drier ☐
deep freeze ☐
drying rack ☐
dustpan and brush ☐
broom ☐
shelving ☐
toolset ☐
paint and decorating items ☐
ladder ☐
workbench ☐

## ★ *PERSONAL*
wedding clothes ☐
nightclothes ☐
night in honeymoon suite ☐

## ★ *LEISURE AND PLEASURE*
backgammon set ☐
card table ☐
playing card set ☐
camera ☐
videocamera ☐
health club membership ☐
luggage ☐

## ★ *STUDY*
desk ☐
chair ☐

shelving .................................................. ☐
filing cabinet .......................................... ☐
angle lamp ............................................. ☐
phone ................................................... ☐
typewriter .............................................. ☐
computer ............................................... ☐

★ *HALL*
shelf ..................................................... ☐
hatrack .................................................. ☐
doormat ................................................. ☐
coat cupboard ........................................ ☐
keyrack ................................................. ☐
mirror .................................................... ☐
table ..................................................... ☐
telephone .............................................. ☐
address book .......................................... ☐
clothes brush .......................................... ☐
shoe cleaning set ..................................... ☐
(See also **Engagement Gifts**.)

## DELIVERING GIFTS AT THE WEDDING

It is preferable for guests to send gifts and cheques in
advance to British weddings. However, as a guest you
will need to take money with you (clean notes), to
French, Italian, Spanish, Greek and Japanese weddings.
The French bride auctions her garter, or is paid for
raising it inch by inch up her leg. The Greek bride has
money pinned on her dress. In Italy and Spain at
wedding receptions guests cut pieces off the groom's
tie, paying money which is given to the bride. Guests
also sign their names inside the bride's shoe and pay
her for the privilege. For Japanese brides the usual gift
is money, wrapped in pretty coloured envelopes.

## GIFT DISPLAY

The bride should list gifts received and thanks sent. Organize the wedding gifts display at home, or in the hotel. Check insurance and security of gifts delivered to the reception hall or hotel. Arrange for the transport of gifts to the new home, perhaps by a security firm. Gifts should be moved promptly so that they are not unattended when the meal starts and do not need moving at the end of the evening.

## THANK YOU GIFTS

Select thank you gifts for the best man, attendants, and bride's mother. Gifts for small bridesmaids could be dolls (Cindy, etc.) which wear many outfits including a wedding dress. Small reproductions of the Royal Family in wedding outfits are available from toy stores. So are plush dolls and bears wearing bridesmaids' dresses. These can be made to order with a reproduction of the bride's wedding dress or the bridesmaids' own dresses. Take a Polaroid photograph of wedding clothing, or save surplus material from the bride's dress hem, to help the toymaker.

Lockets, bracelets, or musical jewellery boxes are also popular. A teenage bridesmaid might like a mirrored make-up case with a light, ear-rings, a matching jewellery set of necklace and bracelet, a pendant, or a travel hairdryer. Pageboys could be given watches.

Gift for (name) ................................................................................................

Purchased from (Store name) ..............................................................

Address ...............................................................................................................

.......................................................................... Tel. ....................................

**Item chosen** ...............................................................................................

**Gift for (name)** .......................................................................................

**Purchased from (Store name)** ............................................................

**Address** ....................................................................................................

........................................................................ **Tel.** ............................

**Item chosen** ...............................................................................................

# THE HONEYMOON

Choose a suitable honeymoon destination you will both enjoy, such as one based on shared interests like hiking or scuba diving. After the excitement of the wedding day you might like to spend a night in your new home. An airport hotel is convenient if you are travelling abroad early next day. Or if you have a long drive, for example from London to the Lake District, stay at a hotel near the reception.

## UK WEDDING NIGHT IN RECEPTION HOTEL

Many hotels offer a free bedroom for the bride and groom if they have a sizeable catered reception held in the hotel. In addition or instead obtain a dressing or changing room in the hotel for daytime use. Luggage can be delivered to the hotel the day before if it is nearby.

## WEDDING NIGHT AT ANOTHER UK HOTEL

Hotels with numerous reception rooms or several rooms with four-poster beds may have as many as five brides arriving on a Saturday evening. The check-in process can be speeded up if the best man goes ahead to deal with the receptionist and handles the luggage. If the bride has made the booking she should have noted in a handbag diary the date her booking was made, with whom and the quality of room promised. Better still carry the confirmation letter. Correspondence shows the name in which she made the booking. This helps sort out confusion when the bride has booked the bedroom in her maiden name, and the couple arrive expecting a room to be listed under their new married name.

Make sure the hotel room has a double bed. Even if you book a double bed there is not much you can do if when you arrive all double-bedded rooms are occupied. You are safest at a hotel where every room has double beds, such as a Holiday Inn. Book a hotel bedroom without a TV set if the groom is likely to spend most of the honeymoon night watching Match of the Day.

Budget honeymoon hotels in the UK, including inexpensive guest houses with four-poster beds, can be found through tourist boards. UK bridal suites can be found in the brochures of hotel groups or from reference books. Hotel wedding packages may include four-posters, jacuzzis, champagne, chocolates, flowers, a greetings card, and a porcelain gift. If no honeymoon package is available, have flowers, champagne, fruit and chocolates delivered to the room. Use Interflora, the hotel's shop and room service, or local shops.

## SELECTING DESIRABLE DESTINATIONS ABROAD

European castles, French chateaux, Spanish paradores, and Portuguese pousadas are romantic. Heart-shaped baths are available at Niagara Falls, Canada, and Couples resorts in Pennsylvania, USA.

Travel agents can recommend tour operators who offer honeymoon options. Companies such as New Beginnings organize Caribbean honeymoons and weddings. They tell you the cost and documentation required. In the Bahamas weddings can take place on beaches, or in the sea with the groom wearing a white Tuxedo (tail-coat) and shorts. The cost of the airport hotel, car parking, or transfer by train to the airport is included in some holiday packages.

Travel agent .......................................................................................

Tourist board .......................................................................................

Airline/shipping company ...............................................................

Airport/Ferry port .............................................................................

Hire car company ...............................................................................

Bank ......................................................................................................

Travellers' Cheques ordered ............................................................

Insurance .............................................................................................

Vaccinations .......................................................................................

Passport office ...................................................................................

Hotel ....................................................................................................

Honeymoon suite/double bed requested No/Yes. Availability confirmed No/Yes. Honeymoon package gifts: Champagne No/Yes. Flowers No/Yes. Fruit No/Yes. Chocolates No/Yes. Others ...................................

........................................................................................ No/Yes.

# HAPPY EVER AFTER

## MARRIAGE ANNOUNCEMENTS IN NEWSPAPERS

Announcements in *The Times*, *The Daily Telegraph* and *The Independent* follow the same format. To have the announcement of a Saturday wedding in the Monday edition of *The Times* you must send in the notice by the preceding Friday. Sample wordings:

MARRIAGES
Mr R. B. King
and Miss J. Hall
The marriage took place on Saturday March 26th, at St George's Church, Hanover Square, of Mr Romeo Bates King, and Miss Juliet Hall.
The Revd Edmund England officiated.
The bride, who was given in marriage by her father, was attended by Miss Anne King. Mr Ashley Jones was best man. A reception was held at The Savoy and the honeymoon is being spent abroad.

Mr R. Brown
and Mrs C. Smith
The marriage took place on Monday, January 1st, at Chelsea Register Office, of Mr R. Brown and Mrs Cecily Smith.

(The title Mrs conveys the information that she is widowed or divorced.)

The Revd A. B. Smith
and Mrs V. A. Brown
The marriage took place at Camden Town Hall, followed by a Service of Blessing conducted by The Revd Thomas Windsor, at St Pancras Church, on December 1st, between Mr Albert Bland Smith and Mrs Verity Anna Brown. A family reception was held at 13 High Square, London WC1.

Shorter versions may appear. For example in *The Independent*:

Montagu/Capulet. On Jan 1st. Romeo to Juliet.

In *The Times*:

Mr B. Smith
and Mrs A. Brown
The marriage took place Monday, January 1st, at Chelsea Register Office of Mr B. Smith and Mrs A. Brown.

Local papers have chattier announcements with photographs. For example:

WEDDING BELLS
Mongagu–Smith
A honeymoon in Italy followed the marriage of Romeo Montagu to Juliet Smith at St Michael's Roman Catholic Church, Harrow Weald.
The bridegroom is the son of Patrick and Maria Montagu of Kingston and the bride is the daughter of John and Ann Smith of Harrow.
The couple will live in Harrow.
Photo: Peter Watford Photography.

National newspaper name .....................................................

Address .........................................................................

......................................................... Tel. .........................

Cost ...............................................................................

Copy deadline date ..........................................................

Publication date ..............................................................

Local newspaper name ......................................................

Address .........................................................................

......................................................... Tel. .........................

Copy deadline ...............................................................

Date published ...............................................................

Reprints of newspaper photos cost .....................................

## PERSONAL MARRIAGE ANNOUNCEMENTS

Order printed business cards and business letterheads, home stationery letterheads, postcards, change of address cards and address stickers. The bank will require a note of the new name and address, also copies of the new signature.

## THE NEW HOME

Arrange transport from the airport to your new home, perhaps a chauffeur-driven limousine. The couple might be welcomed at the airport or at the new home by their parents and chief bridesmaid. Food and flowers left over from the wedding can be placed in the new home. Door keys and security arrangements should have been arranged before departure.

Show the honeymoon film to the wedding hosts and selected guests at a family dinner. Pass around the wedding photo album. An effective audio-visual show can be made showing wedding slides accompanied by music you played at reception (see page 104), then honeymoon slides with evocative regional or national music.

Traditionally, the bride sends out new address cards plus an At Home card inviting guests to call round to see her and the new home on a particular date. As well as her husband, her mother, chief bridesmaid, or sister can help with catering and greeting newcomers while she is showing guests around.

## ORGANIZING YOUR NAME CHANGE

Information on the bride's new names and address and specimen signatures may be required by banks, credit card companies, building societies, mortgage company, landlord, life assurance, car insurance, the Inland Revenue, Department of Social Security, and children's and stepchildren's schools. A new will should be made.

Bank .................................................................................................

Credit cards .................................................................................

Landlord .........................................................................................

Insurance .......................................................................................

Tax office .......................................................................................

DSS ...................................................................................................

School .............................................................................................

Others including the doctor, dentist, hairdresser and

local restaurant will also know the bride under her maiden name until informed. If bride and groom merge names, adopting a hyphenated surname such as Smith-Jones, his business contacts must be told. The same applies if he Anglicizes his family name to make it sound better combined with her first name.

Doctor ........................................................................................................

Dentist ........................................................................................................

Hairdresser ........................................................................................................

Restaurant ........................................................................................................

Get a paying-in book for cheques so wedding cheques can be paid into the new joint account. When cheques are made out to the bride's maiden name she writes on the back Pay ... (inserting her married name) and signs her maiden name.

## FIRST ANNIVERSARY

A tier of the wedding cake can be kept for a baby's christening or the first wedding anniversary. Save the list of wedding guests in order to invite them to happy anniversary celebrations. Remembering anniversaries and birthdays is important if you want to stay happily married.

Anniversary date ........................................................................................

Her parents' anniversary date ........................................................................

His parents' anniversary date ........................................................................

Bride's birthday ........................................................................................

Groom's birthday ........................................................................................

Interflora tel. ..................................   Send fruit tel. ..................

Send rose tel. ............................................. Send tie tel. ......................

Send cake tel. ............................... Send chocs tel. ......................

Department store tel. ......................................................................

Telemessage tel. .............................................................................

# INDEX

Accommodation for wedding guests, 53
Anglo-Catholic weddings, 67
Attendants, choosing, 38–44

Bahai weddings, 72
Banns, marriage, 60, 64
Best man, 35, 36, 38, 40
   responsibilities, 40–2
   speech by, 40, 41, 95–6
   stag party arranged by, 57–9
   thank-you gift to, 114
   transport, 77, 78
   wedding day clothes, 45
Baptist Church, 67
Birthstones, 21
Bride:
   accessories, 44–5
   bouquet, 35, 38, 39, 45
   colour schemes, 37
   going-away outfit, 45
   planning by, 36
   Register Office statement, 63
   trousseau, 35, 36
   wedding dress, 36, 44
Bridegroom:
   engagement gift/wedding ring, 22
   expenses of, 35–6, 38
   organization by, 36
   Register Office statement by, 63
   speech, 95
   stag party, 57–9
   transport, 77, 78
   wedding day clothes, 45
Bride's father, 35, 37, 48, 95
Bride's mother, 35, 36, 46, 114
Bridegroom's father, 95
Bridegroom's mother, 46
Bridesmaids, 36, 37–8
   chief bridesmaid's responsibilities,
     38–9
   gifts for, 114

   wedding day outfits, 46
Buddhist weddings, 73
Budget celebration, 85

Catering, 36
   professional, 84–6
   self-catering, 87–8
Chief bridesmaid, 38–9, 96
Children at wedding reception, 49, 91
Church of England weddings, 60, 64–6
   choosing church music, 65
   guard of honour, 65
   second marriage for divorcee, 66
   widows and widowers, 65–6
Church of Scotland (Presbyterians), 66
Civil marriage, 60–4
   *see also* Register Office
Clothes/dress:
   bride's, 44–5
   bridesmaids, 46
   groom, best man and ushers, 45–6
   hiring, 44, 45, 47
   Irish, 66–7
   mother and mother-in-law, 46
   pageboys, 46
   Scottish, 66
   wedding day, 44–7
   who pays for what?, 37–8
Colour schemes, 37

Dancing, 103
   'last waltz', 104
Decree Nisi, 62
Diamond rings, 19, 20
Disco music, 103–4
Divorce, divorcees, 51, 62, 66, 70
Drinks, 86

Engagement, 18–30
   groom's engagement gift/wedding ring,
     22
   newspaper announcement, 18–19

Engagement gifts, 29–30
  groom's, 22
Engagement party, 23–9, 48, 94
  guest list, 24–7
  invitations, 23
  seating, 28–9
Engagement rings, 19–23
  birthstones, 21
  buying, 19
  diamonds, 20
  gold, 19–20
  safety and insurance, 22–3
  second-hand or inherited, 20
  style and setting, 20
Entertainment, 100–4
Estate agents, 33–4
European Christian weddings, 69
European gifts at wedding, 113
European-style receptions, 89–90
European transport decoration, 81–2

Flowers, 35
  bride's bouquet, 35, 38, 39, 45
  bridesmaids' posies, 46
  buttonholes and corsages, 35, 45–6
  church, 35
Free Churches, 67–8

Gold engagement rings, 19–20
Greek weddings, 113
Gretna Green marriages, 63–4, 84–5
Guard of honour, 65

Hair/headdress, bride's, 44
Hindu hosts and guests, 72
Hindu reception, 86
Hindu transport decoration, 82
Honeymoon, 36, 116–18
  abroad, 117–18
  wedding night, 116–17
House-hunting, 33–4

Invitations:
  engagement party, 23
  ordering printed, 50–3
  wedding, 48–57
Irish reception, 85
Irish weddings, 66–7
Israeli transport decoration, 82

Japanese weddings, 73, 113
Jewish weddings, 69-71, 74–5
  reception, 85
  second marriage, 70–1

Kosher food, 85

London Diamond Centre, 19

Maid-of-honour, 39
Marriage:
  abroad, 62
  by certificate, 61
  by certificate and licence, 61
  to a foreigner, 62
  minimum age for, 62
  mixed-faith, 73–4
Marriage announcements:
  in newspapers, 119–21
  personal, 121
Matron-of-honour, 39
Methodist Church, 67–8
*Mikva* (Jewish ritual bath), 70
Mixed-faith marriages, 73–4
Music, 100–4
  choosing church, 65
  dance music volume, 103
  disco, 103–4
  live, 100–1
  national and international, 102–3
  personal songs, 101
  recorded, 104
  regional, 102
  sentimental, 101–2
  wedding theme songs, 101
Muslim/Islamic weddings, 71–2
Muslim reception, 85–6
Muslim transport decoration, 82

Name change, organizing, 122–3
National Association of Goldsmiths, 19
New home, 33–5, 121–2
Newspaper announcements:
  engagement, 18
  marriage, 119–21
Nonconformist weddings, 67, 73

Pageboys, 114
  wedding-day outfits, 46
Pentecostal Church, 67
Photographs, 41, 97–9
  amateur, 97
  professional, 98–9

Quaker weddings, 67, 68–9

Register Office marriage, 39, 60–4, 75–6
  Bahai weddings, 72
  by certificate, 61
  by certificate and licence, 61
  marriage statement, 63
  in Scotland, 63
  second marriage, 62

who can marry whom?, 62
Religious ceremonies, 64–75
    Anglo-Catholic, 67
    Bahais, 72
    Buddhist, 73
    Church of England, 64–6
    Church of Scotland, 66
    European Christian weddings, 69
    Hindu, 72
    Irish weddings, 66–7
    Jewish weddings, 69–71, 74–5
    Methodist, 67–8
    mixed-faith marriages, 73–4
    Muslim weddings, 71–2, 75
    Nonconformist and Free Churches, 67
    Oriental, 73
    Quaker weddings, 68–9
    Roman Catholic, 67, 74
    Sikh, 72
Rings:
    engagement, 19–23
    groom's, 22
    wedding, 41
Roman Catholic weddings, 67, 74

Scotland, 62
    Bahai wedding, 72
    Church of Scotland, 66
    Register Office marriage, 63–4
    wedding receptions, 84–5
Seating plans:
    engagment party, 28–9
    wedding reception, 91
Second marriage, 36, 60, 62, 66
    Jewish, 70–1
    printed invitations, 51–2
Sikh ceremonies, 72
Special Licence, 62
Speeches and toasts, 41, 58, 95–6
Stag/hen party, 57, 94
    entertainment – spoof speeches, 58
    fancy dress parties at home, 59
    transport home, 58
    venues, 57
Student marriages, 32

Table decoration, 90–1
Telegrams, reading out, 41
Toastmasters, 93
Transport, 41, 77–83
    to church/Register Office, 77
    coping with practical jokes, 80
    departure car, 35, 79
    European/foreign decoration of cars,
        81–2

going away car, 79–80
guests' arrival, 77
hiring cars, 77
home after stag/hen party, 58
payment of, 35
to reception, 78–9
taxi/bus, 78–9

United Reformed Church, 67
Ushers, 35, 36, 38, 40, 41
    responsibilities, 42–4
    wedding day clothes, 45

Veil, bride's, 44
Videotaping, 99–100

Wedding album, 9, 122
Wedding anniversary, first, 123
Wedding cake, 89, 123
    cutting, 94
Wedding calendar, 10–17
Wedding dress, 35, 44
Wedding gifts, 106–15
    checklist, 107–13
    delivering at wedding, 113
    display, 114
    making lists, 106
    store gift list, 106–7
    thank-you, 114
Wedding guests, 48–57
    additions and deletions, 50
    arranging accommodation for, 53
    children, 49
    costs, 48–9
    equal numbers of relatives from each
        side, 49
    how many?, 48–9
    lists of, 54–7
    ordering printed invitations, 50–3
    transport to meet, 77
Wedding night in UK hotels, 116–17
Wedding reception, 48–57, 84–105
    accommodation for guests, 53
    at home, 88–9
    budget celebration, 87
    cake cutting, 94
    children at, 49
    costs/payment of, 35, 36, 48–9
    dancing, 103
    delivering gifts at foreign, 113
    disco music, 103–4
    drinks, 86
    entertainment, 100–4
    European-style, 88–90

ordering printed invitations, 50–3
photographs, 97–9
planning, 84–105
professional catering, 84–6
recorded music, 104
in Scotland, 84–5
seating plans, 91–3
self-catering, 87–8
speeches, 95–6
table decoration, 90–1
toastmasters, 93
videotaping, 99–100
wedding cake, 89, 90

where to hold, 84
Wedding ring, 41
Weddings, 31–47
  autumn and winter, 32
  choosing attendants, 38–44
  clothes, 44–7
  colour schemes, 37
  date of, 31–2
  summer, 31–2
  weekday vs. weekend, 33
  who pays for clothes, 37–8
  who pays for what, 35–6
Widows and widowers, 51, 65–6

## THE FAMILY MATTERS SERIES

**Anniversary Celebrations** 0 7063 6636 0
**Baby's First Year** 0 7063 6778 2
**Baby's Names and Star Signs** 0 7063 6801 0
**Baby's Names** 0 7063 6542 9
**Card Games** 0 7063 6635 2
**Card Games for One** 0 7063 6747 2
**Card and Conjuring Tricks** 0 7063 6811 8
**Charades and Party Games** 0 7063 6637 9
**Children's Party Games** 0 7063 6611 5
**Dreams and Their Meanings** 0 7063 6802 9
**Early Learning Games** 0 7063 6771 5
**Handwriting Secrets Revealed** 0 7063 6841 X
**How to be the Best Man** 0 7063 6748 0
**Microwave Tips and Timings** 0 7063 6812 6
**Modern Etiquette** 0 7063 6641 7
**Naming Baby** 0 7063 5854 6
**Palmistry** 0 7063 6894 0
**Successful Children's Parties** 0 7063 6843 6
**Travel Games** 0 7063 6643 3
**Wedding Etiquette** 0 7063 6868 1
**Wedding Planner** 0 7063 6867 3
**Wedding Speeches and Toasts** 0 7063 6642 5